D0629212

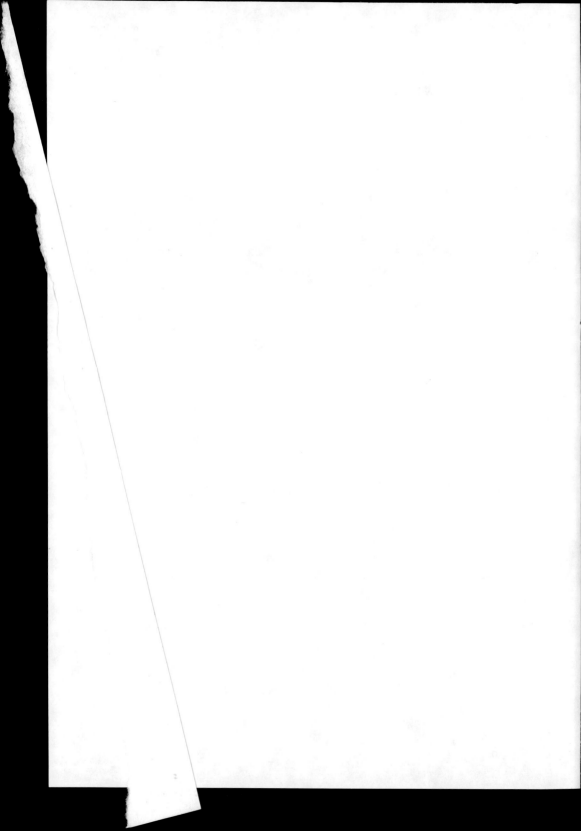

Breaking the Word

Essays on the
Liturgical Dimensions of Preaching

edited by Carl P. Daw, Jr.

Church Hymnal Corporation • New York

The Church Hymnal Corporation
445 Fifth Avenue
New York, NY 10016

Contents

Editor's Note

THE ESSAYS IN THIS VOLUME have all been written specifically for this collection and appear here for the first time, with the exception of the one by John Snow. His essay was especially edited from its original publication as the chapter on preaching in his book, *The Impossible Vocation: Ministry in the Mean Time* (Cambridge, MA: Cowley Publications, 1988), pp. 73–91. It appears here by permission of the author and of the publisher.

To all this talented, articulate, and distinguished company I am most grateful for their cooperation and diligence in producing these varied and complementary essays, as well as their patience in the lapse between submission and publication. Though there are clearly some differences of approach or emphasis among the writers appearing here, the truly remarkable feature of their contributions is a spirit of enthusiasm for the power and promise of preaching. Each of the essays offered here contains some insight, information, or perspective that will enhance the preaching of those who turn to them for help and encouragement. While few people might choose to read straight through this book at one

Carl P. Daw, Jr.   v sitting, it is hoped that it will prove a collection to which preachers will return from time to time for renewed understanding and direction.

I am thankful to our publisher, Frank Hemlin, for his enthusiasm for this project and his perseverance in getting it into print. As always, I am indebted to my wife, May Bates Daw, for unflagging support, judicious evaluations, and scrupulous proofreading. Any typographical errors that remain are probably something I added that she didn't see.

Carl P. Daw, Jr.

Introduction

Breaking the Word: A Liturgical Rationale for Preaching

Carl P. Daw, Jr.

Break thou the bread of life, dear Lord, to me,
as thou didst break the loaves beside the sea;
beyond the sacred page I seek thee, Lord,
my spirit pants for thee, O living Word.

THOUGH THE FIRST HALF of this opening stanza of Mary Artemisia Lathbury's hymn might seem to imply Communion, the latter half clearly attests to its origins as a prayer for Bible study groups at the Chautauqua Assembly, where it has been sung for over a century at Sunday vesper services. Episcopalians who know this hymn will have learned it in other churches, for it has never appeared in an Episcopal hymnal. Yet it captures well a widespread and enduring Christian understanding that we find nourishment from what Augustine called "the breaking of the Word." As that phrase implies, Christ is made present at every Eucharist not only in the Liturgy of the Table but also in the *anamnesis* of proclamation.

Recovering from Amnesia

Perhaps the greatest impediment to the integration of preaching into liturgical worship is a lingering assumption that the two do not belong together. Like those optical illusions where figure and ground move back and forth between the dark and light portions, our eucharistic liturgies often seem constructed so that either what happens in the pulpit is experienced as a delay in getting to the Table or the receiving of Communion feels like an appendage to the preaching and hearing of the Word. We have a hard time keeping Word and Table balanced and complementary.

To a great extent these assumptions are the remnants of our checkered history. Though it is widely claimed (with some justification) that the current Book of Common Prayer has blurred or even eliminated the former distinctions between the so-called Protestant and Anglo-Catholic wings of the Episcopal Church, some residual attitudes and perspectives remain. These received persuasions are especially evident in our inherited spaces and their furnishings. The positions, proportions, and immobility of our altars, pulpits, and fonts frequently hinder us from carrying out the intentions of the liturgy.[1] Rare indeed is a space that works well in every respect. Like actors trying to prevail over an unsupportive set, those who preside and preach have to overcome the disjunction between the implications of the place and the intentions of the liturgy. Such a gap ultimately eviscerates an incarnational faith.

But it is unlikely that this situation will change markedly in the near future, which means that we must learn to overcome the limitations of our histories as well as their reification in stained glass, stone, brick, and wood. Perhaps living with the consequences of our forebears' good intentions will teach us both humility and caution as we seek to recover the fullness of Christian tradition and hand it on.

Like impoverished gentry who have for generations restricted themselves to ever-smaller portions of a great rambling house, we have truncated our traditions for so long that we do not even know the extent of our heritage. Yet in the excitement of discovering and reclaiming the spaciousness of pre-medieval liturgies or the wealth of biblical images for God, for example, we must be careful not to distort intervening ages into villains and heretics. What we are about is a process of healing and integration, and it cannot be accomplished by any sort of quick fix. It is just as futile to attempt to retreat to the liturgical style of, say, the fourth century of the Christian era as it would be to renounce electricity or central heating. We cannot deny the world in which people live now, but at the same time we need to counteract its reductionist tendencies by opening up for present day Christians what is often an unexpected abundance of scripture, tradition, and human experience. Above all, we carry the good news that this is our very own birthright, held in common with faithful people of every generation and every place. Together we begin to reclaim more than we knew we had forgotten.

A Fourfold Shape for Proclamation

Ever since Dom Gregory Dix elucidated the four-action shape accompanying the bread of the Eucharist (and the corollary three-fold action for the wine), that analysis has been fruitfully employed both in the study of historical rites and in the development of new ones.[2] Following the principal verbs of the institution narrative, those who preside at the Eucharist pattern their actions on Christ's taking, blessing, breaking, and giving of bread. Recognition of this vital skeleton within the liturgy has enabled us to reform and clarify both our rites and our ceremonies remarkably. I believe that this fourfold action also has significant implications for how we approach the proclamation of the Word.

Taking the Word

Jesus took bread; the preacher takes scripture. But it isn't taken at random. By means of an appointed lectionary, the Church has designated which and how much scripture. Preachers in denominations without a lectionary sometimes chide us for presuming to limit God's Word, but anyone who has grappled with a Sunday's full provision of three readings and a psalm can testify that even this relatively small portion of the Bible is more scripture than one preacher can exhaust. It may look at first like only a few loaves, but there is enough here to fill all who seek to be fed.

That Jesus took bread rather than raw wheat also has implications for how the preacher regards that scripture. Bread is the work of human hands and the fruit of human labor. When we bring bread to God's Table, we celebrate our participation in God's creation as well as Christ's sharing in our humanity. In the same way, when we read the story of God's activity in, with, and on behalf of human beings, we interact with it. We knead and flatten and mold it with all the powers of our being and engage it with everything we know and wonder about. To extend the analogy a bit, the vessels and tools we use for this work are the tradition of the Church, which has learned through long experience that, for example, the somewhat lumpy New Testament formula "Father, Son, and Holy Spirit" can be handled with the name-tool "Trinity." Yet we also live in a time when some of the inherited tools no longer feel right in our hands or can no more perform their intended task. When it is harder to do the task with the tool than without it, the time has come to retire the old tool and find a new one. Drawing on the teaching of Gregory of Nyssa, the Orthodox theologian Paul Evdokimov has said, "Tradition is something we find in the past which is in agreement with our future." So the dough of scripture is shaped not only by the tools of tradition but also by the energy of our human experience. In affirming the value of our participation in the revelation of God's word, we do not presume to limit or control but to discern, to interpret, and to transmit.

Blessing the Word

Just as the taking of scripture entails more than its being read for the gathered assembly, so the blessing of the Word involves more than a quick Trinitarian formula in the pulpit. The timeworn principle that sermon preparation should begin, continue, and end in a spirit of prayer is both a beginner's exercise and a counsel of perfection.

Such prayer is not a display of pious passivity. Rather, it draws on the ancient monastic insight that work and prayer form a continuum, or as Simone Weil remarked, "Absolute attention is prayer." Becoming deeply aware of the linguistic nuances and cultural assumptions that shape and color a passage therefore becomes an integral part of praying that God will speak to us through it. Like Moses before the burning bush, we need to stand unshod and in intimate contact with the environment through which God addresses us. Ideally, this means reading scripture in the original language in order to hear its iteration, music, and wordplay. When that is not possible, we need to keep in mind the many limitations of even the best translation. As an ancient Latin proverb puts it, "To translate is to betray." We will have a harder time hearing God speak if we have a faulty interpreter.

Nor does the blessing of the Word presume that we are bestowing worth on something that would be valueless without our intervention. What we pray for is not that meaning will be given but that meaning will be revealed. Indeed, it is our confidence that tradition and experience operate on scripture like the technique of triangulation in surveying: the correlation and combination of openness to tradition and awareness of experience provide a dependable understanding of the truth, wisdom, and love of God conveyed to us through the Bible by the Holy Spirit. Blessing the Word is above all prayer that God's will and purpose may be made present to us so that we may share it with God's people.

Breaking the Word

The objective of breaking bread is to reduce a daunting loaf into pieces capable of being chewed and digested; preaching endeavors to offer people a manageable portion of God's Word to strengthen and sustain them. Some preachers attempt to do this by honing their sermon to one memorable sentence, but this approach is at best uneven and can be counterproductive if it promotes a simplistic and predictable approach to scripture.[3]

One helpful means of making the Word accessible is to find the unifying thread woven through the Propers of the day, even though this is a task that sometimes eludes even the best commentators.[4] Often a return to the original languages will reveal connections obscured by English translations, such as the common root in Greek for the verb "to believe" and the noun "faith," or the shared stems among words for "grace," "joy," and "thanksgiving." On the other hand, preachers should not shrink from expressing honest perplexity in the face of scriptures that seem to lead in various directions. That is, after all, frequently the reaction of people in the congregation, most of whom will not have any clear sense of relationship among the passages they hear read at worship.

In many ways, the lack of connections among the appointed passages or the occurrence of difficult and challenging texts offers the preacher a clear indication of where to break the Word. Such uncomfortable places and question marks operate almost like directions to "open along the dotted line." Especially as we learn to appreciate that the life of faith is not a monolithic and unvaried resolve, it becomes both pastorally desirable and ethically imperative for preachers to indicate that searching, questioning, and doubt are faithful responses to the encounter with scripture. Far more dangerous is the pious apathy that says, in effect, "Whatever is in the Bible is fine with me." How ironic it is that some of the very people who would be irate if Communion were restricted to the clergy seem perfectly content to relegate real engagement with scripture to ordained persons, yet also complain that they "don't get much out of church."

Part of the challenge of breaking the Word therefore becomes to find the parallels and echoes between the scriptures and the lives of one's hearers. This is where the reason/experience component of classic Anglican theology engages the ministry of proclamation. Jesus told us to be "wise as serpents and innocent as doves" (Matthew 10:16), but we have generally been more interested in being harmless than in being wily. In particular we might do well to emulate Jesus' own cunningness and humor in applying scripture to everyday life; the "render unto Caesar" pericope (Mark 12:13–17 and parallels), for example, is no less valuable for its method than for its precept. If we are responsive to the questions of our hearers—both the actual ones and the implicit ones, they will help us break the Word rightly and well.

Giving the Word

The familiar petition in the Prayer for the Whole State of Christ's Church that "this congregation here present . . . may hear and receive [God's] holy Word" (BCP, p. 329) has been worn so smooth by much hearing that we may not heed its double force: for the congregation to receive God's holy Word requires that it be given to them. Preachers have a sacred responsibility to deliver their sermons with no less care than that expected of those who distribute the consecrated elements of the Eucharist.

An effective sermon is not the same thing as a vocalized essay: preaching involves far more than reading a script without losing one's place or mispronouncing anything. Though extravagant and self-conscious theatricality should obviously be avoided, the qualitative difference between hearing a line said in character and hearing it read from a playtext offers a helpful measure of the contrast between a sermon *delivered* and a sermon *read.* Every congregation has the right to have the Word given to them with the same sense of presence and attention that accompanies the ministration of Communion. Yet clergy who would never countenance the slovenly provision of stale bread or sour wine often show no compunction in nonchalantly serving up homiletic leftovers. We ought to have learned by now that Marshall McLuhan was right in warning us that "the medium is the message": how we proclaim is an inseparable part of what we proclaim.

Though the personal immediacy of serving Communion should be emulated in the delivery of a sermon, it should also be noted that attempting to be too personal can backfire.[5] More than one tyro preacher has come to grief by trying to use a sermon as a means of dealing with a particular parishioner's problems. I can still remember far too well my own searing experience as a seminarian in preparing a sermon for my fieldwork parish that I thought would be the perfect way of communicating to a certain troubled parishioner exactly what she needed to hear, only to discover that she wasn't in church that Sunday! In hindsight I came to regard her absence as providential, because preaching that sermon with the private goal of dealing with only one person's issues would not have been justifiable even if she had been present, any more than it would have been excusable to allow her to be the only one to receive Communion.

The delivery of the sermon is an opportunity to celebrate the shared immediacy of worship and to inculcate an awareness of the corporateness of our life in Christ. The breaking of bread for Eucharist was understood as a sign of participation long before it came to be regarded as a reminder of Christ's brokenness upon the cross.[6] In recovering this attitude in our contemporary celebrations, we find a valuable model for how we are to proclaim the Word. If preachers understand themselves as breaking the Word in and for a community of believers, they can in fact redeem the idiom of "sharing" from being a sentimental and presumptuous euphemism for "telling" and restore it to its rightful sense of mutual participation. When preachers faithfully seek to convey the availability and sufficiency of the proclaimed Word for all members of the Body of Christ, they will find both a freedom and an energy in their expression that they did not enjoy when they regarded their hearers as merely an assembly of individuals.

Twelve Baskets of Leftovers

The parallels between the Liturgy of the Word and the Liturgy of the Table should not be carried to the point of trying to consume any remaining elements before leaving. Don't be afraid of leaving loose ends. It is far better for a sermon to end with an honest question than with a hollow affirmation.

If the preacher's task has been done well, the congregation will find themselves with all sorts of fragments of scripture, tradition, and experience to take home with them. Those who preach and those who plan liturgy need to be careful to provide sufficient and appropriate baskets for carrying away this undigested surplus. Though preachers sometimes hate to admit it, people are more likely to leave church humming the last hymn than retracing the outline of the sermon. How very important it then becomes to choose that hymn with great care. In effect, it becomes the vessel for retaining and conveying the experience of worship into the daily lives of worshipers.

Similarly, the hymns, anthems, and prayers that precede and follow the sermon need to be chosen with careful attention. In particular, thoughtful consideration should be given to the compatibility between the Propers and the Eucharistic Prayer. Simply to use Prayer A because it is the first one in the Prayer Book or because it is shorter than others ignores the potential of the Liturgy of the Table to continue and enhance the proclamation of the Liturgy of the Word. Understanding the entire liturgy—rather than simply the sermon—as an occasion of proclamation both reduces the pressure on the preacher and increases the congregation's opportunity to hear and receive the Word. Such effort to make worship a coherent and unified experience is not an aesthetic indulgence but a conscientious commitment to convey by every means possible the conviction that God's redemptive activity in Christ has "brought us out of error into truth, out of sin into righteousness, out of death into life" (BCP, p. 368). This is abundant good news that will always exceed the bounds of our sermons and our liturgies, and it will nourish us through all our days.

Notes:

1. See Marion J. Hatchett, "The Architectural Implications of the Book of Common Prayer" [Occasional Paper Number Seven (March 1985)] in *The Occasional Papers of the Standing Liturgical Commission: Collection Number One* (New York: Church Hymnal Corporation, 1987), pp. 57–66; and Carl P. Daw, Jr., "The Exegesis of Liturgical Space," *Open*, March 1987, 1–11.

2. *The Shape of the Liturgy* (London: A. & C. Black, 1945; rpt. New York: Seabury Press, 1982); see especially the notes to the Seabury edition by Paul Marshall, pp. 765–766, for studies of Dix's influence.

3. For an example of the one-sentence method see the "practical application" sections of John F. Craghan, C.SS.R., *Yesterday's Word Today: A Textual Explanation and Practical Application of the Three-Year Sunday-Festal Lectionary* (Collegeville, MN: The Liturgical Press, 1982).

4. Although some of the examples that Reginald H. Fuller cannot reconcile derive from instances where the Roman Catholic lectionary differs from the Episcopal one, it is also the case that our variants can sometimes introduce confusion where there

seemed to be coherence; see his *Preaching the Lectionary: The Word of God for the Church Today*, rev. ed. (Collegeville, MN: The Liturgical Press, 1984).

5. This is true of the ministration of Communion as well. The frequently-encountered practice of adding the communicant's name to the sentence of administration works only if everyone present is known to the minister of Communion. To address some by name and not others is in effect to reduce the unnamed to second-class status and is a breach of charity.

6. Cf. Howard E. Galley, *The Ceremonies of the Eucharist: A Guide to Celebration* (Cambridge, MA: Cowley Publications, 1989), pp. 118–119.

Preaching as
Remembering

The Claiming and Reclaiming of Baptismal Identity

Michael W. Merriman

WHAT IS "BAPTISMAL IDENTITY"? It might seem at first glance to be simply one among many possible Christian identities: Eucharistic identity, priestly identity, evangelical or catholic identity, Anglican identity, or some other label. But it would be a mistake to view this as yet another term of differentiation among Christians. *Baptismal identity is Christian identity.* Yet we find both preachers and those to whom they preach attempting to describe the Christian life with no reference at all to baptism. If preaching is to be restored to vigor in the Church, if it is to have power to equip the People of God for living and ministering in the world, it must once again enable them to claim their baptism as the essential context of their identity.

"Once again," because there was a time when our adoption as sons and daughters by water and the Holy Spirit was definitive for being Christian. The ancient theologians such as Ambrose, Augustine, John Chrysostom, Cyril of Jerusalem, Cyprian of Carthage, Basil, and Gregory of Nazianzus did a great part of their theology in sermons and catechesis about baptism. Today, however, it is quite possible to hear baptism mentioned in a sermon only at baptismal liturgies, if then. This silence about baptism represents not only a loss of our connection with an essential Christian understanding of former ages but also a failure to live out the assumptions of our own contemporary articulation of Christian faith and practice, as set forth in our current Book of Common Prayer.

How Does the Prayer Book Understand Baptism?

The Book of Common Prayer presents baptism as "full initiation by water and the Holy Spirit into Christ's Body the Church" (p. 298). It is so central that it is to be "administered within the Eucharist as the chief service on a Sunday or other feast." Its normal minister is the bishop. Its celebration is to be limited, so far as is possible, to only the most solemn occasions: Easter, Pentecost, All Saints, the Baptism of Christ, and the bishop's visitation. The Eucharist is not presented as a possible option in the service but rather its normal context, for the prayer book regards the Eucharist as one of the three parts of Christian Initiation: baptism, sealing, and participation in the Eucharistic feast. The Eucharist is the repeatable part of baptism.

It is, however, the case that many if not most clergy and lay people have failed to notice what the prayer book says about baptism. In many cases the liturgical piety surrounding baptism is still that of the Medieval Church. Baptism is seen as a personal event, not a community event; as a preliminary to more important events such as Confirmation, first Communion, or Ordination; as a special ministry to babies and an occasional and somewhat embarrassing event for adults.

The Baptismal Rite makes it clear, however, that baptism is a community event in which individuals become members of a household and a heritage: a community which is eternal and rooted in God. It is quite specific in stating that baptism is "full initiation . . ." It is not preliminary to anything, but conveys the fullness of Christian life and ministry. It is primarily a ministry of the community which is adult in nature and requires full maturity and formation of the adult candidates and of the sponsors and parents of young children.

One bishop has pointed out the visual sign of one aspect of this failure to understand baptism as it is described in the Book of Common Prayer by drawing attention to the certificates given for baptism (very small and plain) with those for ordination (large, colorful, and suitable for framing). Our fonts are often tucked away in obscure corners, making them both difficult to use in a congregational setting and ineffective as constant reminders of our essential baptismal identity. Furthermore, they seldom hold enough water to permit anyone—even a baby—to be immersed, thereby eliminating the effective enactment of burial and resurrection which the prayer book rite assumes. Another sign of our minimalization of baptism is the failure of preachers much of the time regularly and consistently to relate the Gospel and its way of living in Christ to baptism.

Baptism and Christian Living

It is true that many clergy and other teachers are excited about the promises in the Baptismal Covenant (pp. 304–5) as ways of describing Christian living. However we are less likely to hear proclaimed the baptismal liturgy's description of who we are as baptized people. Attention to the liturgical texts, especially to the verbs used, can be revealing. The baptized are:

Delivered from the way of sin and death
Their hearts are *opened* to God's grace and truth
They are *filled* with God's holy and life-giving Spirit
They are *kept* by God in the faith and communion of the
  Church
Taught to love others in the power of the Spirit
Sent into the world in witness to God's love
Brought to the fullness of God's peace and glory
Baptized into the death of Jesus Christ that they may
live in the power of his resurrection and
look for him to come in glory
Buried with Christ in his death

Michael W. Merriman

17

Share in his resurrection
Reborn by the Holy Spirit
Bringing others into his fellowship
God has *bestowed* on us the forgiveness of sin
God has *raised* us to new life
God *sustains* us by the gifts of the Holy Spirit
We are *sealed* by the Holy Spirit and *marked* as Christ's own
    forever
We are *received* into the household of God
We *confess* the faith of Christ crucified, *proclaim* his
    resurrection,
and *share* in his eternal priesthood.

It is because of baptism, not good intentions or strong willpower or positive thinking or successful therapy, that the actions described by these verbs are characteristic of Christian people and characteristic of God's actions toward us. Whenever the preacher has occasion to use these verbs, their use in baptism needs to be emphasized.

If one remembers that the Eucharist is part of baptism and that it and all other liturgical rites flow from baptism, then one can engage in a similar exploration of all those other liturgical texts and discover their baptismal orientation. It is not often noticed, for example, that the ordination rites require that deacons being ordered priest and priests being ordered bishop are to be vested only in an alb or surplice without stole or other vestment or insignia of office: in other words, the person is vested as a baptized person. Baptism takes precedence over any other subsequent ecclesiastical office.

The preacher also needs to keep in mind the other texts used in liturgical rites: the psalms and readings, and the hymns. It is to be hoped that preachers will ask themselves during their preparation how the central theme of the sermon relates to baptism. What passages in the readings, in the texts of the liturgy, and in the hymns and anthems are illustrative of what God has done for us in baptism; of how God calls us to live in our baptism; of how baptism helps us to live out our Baptismal Covenant? Such preparation can make sermons come alive, will renew the hearers' commitment, and will reorient their awareness of being part of a community with a story to tell and ministry to do.

Baptismal Themes in the Lectionary

The lectionary is our greatest resource. Although we often fail to notice, it is filled with passages that relate to baptism. Some examples: In Good Friday's reading from Hebrews, does the preacher find reason to refer to baptism?

> "Therefore since we have confidence to enter the sanctuary by the blood of Jesus, by the new and living way which he opened for us through the curtain, that is, through his flesh, and since we have a great priest over the house of God, let us draw near with a true heart in full assurance of faith, with our hearts sprinkled clean from an evil conscience and our bodies washed with pure water . . ."

Or again on Good Friday, the relationship of the piercing of Jesus' side in the Passion reading and the insight given by hymn 165:

> ". . . from that holy body broken
> blood and water forth proceed:
> earth, and stars, and sky, and ocean,
> by that flood from stain are freed."

This hymn's allusion to the traditional understanding of the Johannine streams of blood and water as emblems of eucharist and baptism is likely to be lost on many worshipers unless it is mentioned in the sermon. (Indeed, the Hymnal is full of texts with baptismal imagery; for some representative examples, see the list appended to this essay.) Similarly, the preacher has a splendid opportunity to show how each of the readings in the Great Vigil of Easter—from the waters of creation to Zephaniah's vision of the gathering of God's people renewed in God's love—is a baptismal reading.

Good Friday and the Great Vigil of Easter are fairly obvious sources of baptismal imagery. But let us also look through the readings and other texts throughout the year. Here are some baptismal texts chosen from the Sunday Lectionary in Year B.

I Advent: "I give thanks . . . that in every way you were enriched in Christ Jesus . . . so that you are not lacking in any spiritual gift, as you await the revealing of our Lord Jesus Christ."

II and II Advent: The Gospel both Sundays is about John the Baptist and the call to repentance and baptism.

Christmas Day: The third Collect is a baptismal Collect. Both readings from Titus are about baptism and living out the baptismal life. The Gospel reading from John speaks of those to whom the Word gave the power to become children of God, who were born of God in baptism.

I Epiphany: This is a primary baptismal day and takes its meaning not merely from the historical event of Jesus' baptism but from the baptisms celebrated on the day (or else the renewal of the Baptismal Covenant which should replace the Nicene Creed when there are no baptismal candidates).

II Epiphany: "You were washed, you were sanctified, you were justified in the name of Jesus Christ and in the Spirit of our God."

V Epiphany: Elisha's raising of the son of the Shunammite woman (breathing his spirit into him) is a baptismal image.

VI Epiphany: Naaman is healed by washing in the Jordan.

VII Epiphany: ". . . God has put his seal upon us and given us his spirit in our hearts as a guarantee." The healing (and forgiving) of the paralytic, lowered through the roof is an image of our descending into the waters of baptism.

I Lent: All three readings. This is, of course, the day when Candidates for Baptism at Easter are enrolled and begin their final preparation. It sets the central theme of all of Lent: Baptism. All the Lenten readings should be seen through the context of baptism, especially those in Year A.

Easter Day: All three Collects are baptismal. "Since you have been raised with Christ, seek the things that are above . . . For you have died, and your life is hid with Christ in God." Renewal of the Baptismal Covenant replaces the Creed when there are no baptisms.

II Easter: "Whatever is born of God overcomes the world; and this is the victory that overcomes the world, our faith. Who is it that overcomes the world but whoever believes that Jesus is the Son of God? This is he who came by water and the blood, Jesus Christ, not with the water only but with the water and the blood." (The account of Thomas on this Sunday is for all the baptized who have lost the first excitement of their baptism.) Like Lent, Eastertide readings should all be seen as related to baptism for this is the time when the Church opens up to the newly baptized and to all the faithful the mysteries of the faith into which we were baptized.

Vigil of Pentecost: The Gospel reading of Christ, the source of living waters.

The Day of Pentecost: This is a major baptismal feast. The Collects and Proper Preface are baptismal. "I will pour water on the thirsty land, and streams on the dry ground; I will pour my Spirit upon your descendants . . ." "For by one Spirit we were all baptized into one body . . ." The Baptismal Covenant should be renewed in place of the Nicene Creed when there are no baptisms.

Trinity Sunday: The Gospel is Jesus' conversation with Nicodemus concerning rebirth "by water and the Spirit."

Proper 4: ". . . always carrying in the body the death of Jesus, so that the life of Jesus may also be manifested in our bodies . . ."

Proper 5: ". . . knowing that he who raised the Lord Jesus will raise us also with Jesus and bring us with you into his presence . . ."

Proper 7: ". . . Therefore, if anyone is in Christ, there is a new creation; the old has passed away, behold, the new has

Michael W. Merriman   21

come. All this is from God, who through Christ reconciled us to himself . . ." In the Gospel reading Jesus calms the storm on the sea.

Proper 10: ". . . In Christ you also, who have heard the word of truth, the gospel of your salvation, and have believed in him, were sealed with the promised Holy Spirit, which is the guarantee of our inheritance . . ."

Proper 11: The Gospel reading of the feeding of the 5,000 is eucharistic and, hence, baptismal.

Proper 12: At the Jordan, Elijah commissions Elisha as prophet after him and is taken up. The obvious Exodus imagery of each prophet parting Jordan's waters is a baptismal image. The second reading in this proper is, ". . . There is one body and one Spirit, just as you were called to the one hope that belongs to your call, one Lord, one faith, one baptism . . ." And the Gospel finds Jesus again calming the sea.

Propers 13–16: The Gospels are the Bread of Life discourse and they and the readings are filled with baptismal, eucharistic, and passover images.

Proper 18: The reading from Isaiah uses images of healing and of the desert coming alive with water. The Gospel reading is the healing of the deaf-mute. "Ephphatha" is a classic baptismal term referring to the new life given us in Christ, in hearing and proclaiming the Word.

Proper 22: ". . . it was fitting that he, for whom and by whom all things exist, in bringing many children to glory, should make the pioneer of their salvation perfect through suffering. For he who sanctifies and those who are sanctified have all one origin . . ."

Proper 24: The sons of Zebedee seek places of honor in Christ's glory. This is a baptismal reading.

Proper 25: The reading from Hebrews is for catechumens and those who continue to be formed into their baptismal life. The

Gospel reading is the healing of blind Bartimaeus. Baptism is often called "enlightenment" in Christian tradition. It heals our spiritual blindness.

All Saints: In both second readings terms such as "sealed," "white robes," "washed," "living water," "guarantee," and "eyes of your hearts enlightened" are all baptismal terms. The Baptismal Covenant replaces the Nicene Creed when there are no baptismal candidates.

Proper 28: In the reading from Hebrews we are called to remember "the former days when, after you were enlightened, you endured a hard struggle . . ." This refers to living out our baptismal life.

Proper 29: ". . . To him who loves us and has freed us from our sins by his blood and made us a kingdom, priests to his God and Father . . ."

This is a cursory survey of the readings and a few liturgical texts from only one year in the three-year lectionary cycle. It should be clear from these examples that the lectionary gives us ample opportunity for holding up baptism and its effects in the life of the community of faith when we proclaim the Word in the sermon. Indeed, there is a sense in which every sermon should proclaim baptism.

Connecting Sermons with Baptism

Sermons often urge the faithful to renewed commitment to God and ministry to others. Preachers should not assume that the connection will be made between baptism and commitment or between ministry and baptism. We need to be reminded that we have been equipped in baptism to turn to God and to minister in Christ's name to others. Otherwise our exhortations will be pelagian calls to earn salvation by good works rather than calls to become what God has made us to be in baptism.

We need sermons that articulate what it means to be members of the household of God. Preachers must call the faithful to confess the faith of Christ crucified and to proclaim his resurrection. Our sermons need to help us discover what it means to share in Christ's eternal priesthood.

The effectiveness of sermons is lessened if the liturgical rites within which they are preached are carelessly planned or if they fail to use and take seriously the words, actions, and signs which belong to them. Liturgical reform always seeks to enhance the effectiveness of the proclamation of the Word. Cranmer and Luther knew that a reformed Christianity had to be rooted in a strong baptismal consciousness. Luther told his followers to begin everyday by signing themselves with the Cross and saying, "I am a baptized person." Cranmer required in the first Prayer Book that baptism be celebrated publicly rather than privately. The liturgical renewal in our own century has focused increasingly on the recovery of a full and complete period of preparation for baptism (the Catechumenate) and a full and expressive use of the sacramental signs in the initiation rite.

Private, anonymous celebrations using mere dabs of water and neglecting other symbols make it difficult for preachers or congregation to hear baptismal references when they occur in the liturgical texts and in the scriptures. People who regularly experience full, rich baptismal celebrations will be much more aware of what is happening. For example, in the case of the reading from Revelation on All Saints Day, people who are used to a full baptismal rite—one in which candidates are buried in living (*i.e.* flowing) water; sealed and anointed with fragrant chrism, the sign of the Cross, and the laying on of hands; clothed in a white robe; presented with a candle lighted from the Paschal Candle; and fed (even if they are infants) with the Sacrament of the Eucharistic Banquet—can and will understand that passage as it was originally intended.

When in our sermons we call the People of God to worship regularly, to work for justice and peace, to be evangelists proclaiming Christ, or to care for the sick and the poor and the helpless, we are calling them to claim their baptismal identity.

Do we remember to root such exhortations in baptism? When people ask why the present Prayer Book prefers standing over kneeling (in Rite II liturgies) do we know the answer? Because, say many of the patristic teachers, the world can then see that Christ is risen because Christ's Body is standing in its baptismal identity. Do we still act as though confirmation or ordination makes ordinary Christians into special Christians as if something is lacking in baptism? If we do, we continue the belittlement of lay members of the Church and our exhortations fall on deaf ears because the people have been taught that as "mere" lay people they are lacking the truly important gifts for ministry.

We need preaching which is "mystagogical"—that is, it opens up the mysteries of life in Christ to those who have been baptized into the life of Christ; preaching which proclaims that God has transformed us from the dominion of the world into God's dominion; preaching which announces that Jesus is not simply a historical figure (who once lived on the earth but now is absent, away in heaven) but that Christ is even now alive, preaching, teaching, healing, forgiving, dying, and rising in our own time and communities in the Body of the baptized, royal priesthood.

As St. Augustine of Hippo said in one of his sermons,

> You are the Body of Christ. In you and through you the work of the incarnation must go forward. You are to be taken: you are to be blessed, broken and distributed; that you may be the means of grace and vehicles of the eternal charity.

Appendix: Some hymns with strong baptismal images

This is by no means an exhaustive listing; there are many other hymns containing baptismal images. All numbers refer to *The Hymnal 1982.*

47	149	199	296	349	522	646	685
51	165	200	297	359	523	649	686
76	166	202	298	425	526	650	689
88	174	204	299	432	528	658	690
116	176	228	308	473	547	663	692
120	177	286	309	506	636	664	697
121	187	294	339	507	637	678	699
139	191	295	343	513	645	679	700

Michael W. Merriman

The Recalling of the Sacred Story

Verna J. Dozier

THE CHARGE TO REMEMBER is a sacred charge.

As the King James Version has it in the sixth chapter of Deuteronomy:

> And when thy son asketh thee in time to come, saying, What mean the testimonies, and the statutes, and the judgments, which the Lord our God hath commanded you?
> Then thou shalt say unto thy son, We were Pharaoh's bondmen in Egypt; and the Lord brought us out of Egypt with a mighty hand.

And the earliest record we have of the institution of the Lord's Supper is in Paul's first letter to the Corinthians in which he said:

> For I received from the Lord what I also delivered to you, that the Lord Jesus on the night when he was betrayed took bread, and when he had given thanks, broke it, and said, "This is my body which is [broken] for you. Do this in remembrance of me." In the same way also the cup, after supper, saying, "This cup is

the new covenant in my blood. Do this, as often as you drink
it, in remembrance of me." (RSV)

I believe that the most important function of the sermon is to recall
the sacred story. Our lectionary gives us a rich resource at every
eucharist to do just that—an Old Testament lesson, a psalm, a
reading from one of the gospels, and a reading from an epistle or
the book of Acts or the Revelation. We have the possibility at
every eucharist to tell the Story.

Why the Story Isn't Told

Unfortunately, this possibility often goes unrealized for three principal reasons, as I see them:

First, we concentrate on the Gospel passage. During Advent,
we may give some attention to the Old Testament lesson, since we
see Advent as an Old Testament time. In Advent then we may
take our text, as it were, from the Old Testament lesson. And
sometimes during the Sundays after Pentecost we may look to the
Epistle for inspiration. We are especially moved to do so if the
lectionary follows one epistle for a succession of Sundays. We may
even be moved to do a series of sermons on the Epistle. Generally,
however, we concentrate on the Gospel for our sermons.

Second, we read the Bible in bits and pieces. We do not encounter the Bible as a totality. We do not see it as a story that begins
with the Creation and ends pointing to the New Creation. Our
educational system has taught us to value answers more than
questions. The most respected members of the educational enterprise were the ones who had the answers, the experienced, the
university-trained, the keepers of the community store of knowledge. The least respected were the young, the visionary, the
questioners. To ask the questions in this mode of education was
the function of the most respected. To give the answers the most
respected already knew was the function of the least respected.
This concept of education we took to our Bible study, and it
became our religious duty to view the Bible as an Answer Book.
Even those of us who balk at subscribing to theories of inerrancy

declare in ordination ceremonies our belief that the Bible is the word of God without giving much thought to what that expression means. We see the Bible as The Answer Book, and we go to it for answers succinctly stated in discrete verses which we can hurl at one another to prove points or mouth easily to take care of the troubled. In our zeal for the parts, we have missed the beauty and grandeur of the whole. I submit to you that the Bible contains the Story, the remarkable Story of the action of God to accomplish God's sovereign will. I submit to you further that no verse, no chapter, no book of the Bible stands by itself. Each verse, each chapter, each book is a part of the total Story. None stands by itself. Each is a part of the total Story. Recalling that Story, I think, is the most important function of the sermon.

Third, the very order of our liturgy militates against our understanding of the Story. The liturgy moves through the Old Testament reading to the New Testament lessons—Epistles or Acts or Revelation. The liturgy climaxes with the reading of the Gospel, for which we have a glorious procession, and the congregation rises to its feet to honor this significant moment. It is exciting liturgy, and I, surprisingly enough, would not change it. It bears witness to the fact that with the Gospel we have reached the climax of the liturgy. It obscures, however, the very important fact that with the Gospel we have reached only the midpoint of the Story. The Story moves on through the other New Testament readings and on into the life of the people of God gathered in that place for Eucharist. The sermon needs to make that point clear.

To these three principal reasons why the Story is not told in our sermons a fourth could be added. This additional reason, alas, is that many of us don't know the Story. I have made it a practice when I work with clergy on developing sermons to begin by asking them to tell the story of the Bible in five sentences. One of the most troubling responses was from a clergyperson who began the Story with Jesus. I do not believe the Story begins with Jesus or ends with Jesus. The Story, I believe, begins with God. The Story continues beyond the pages of the Bible to end with us. The happiest response was from a priest who said immediately, "That's what the Eucharistic prayer does!" In six different ways the

Eucharistic prayers do it. I think, however, it is a discipline all of us must engage in for ourselves; and I believe that the Story as we understand it should be recalled in every sermon that we preach.

What Is the Heart of the Story?

How would I attempt to tell the whole Story in five sentences? Though I believe that one's summary of the Story can change, I would begin my summary now with this statement:

First Sentence: The Story begins with the creation of a good world by a loving God. Three very important affirmations are in that sentence. "In the beginning God." That is the basic Biblical faith. The essence of faith is that it implies risk. We have lost that existential dimension of faith. Faith is not a proposition to be proved, a philosophical thesis to be argued. It is a risk of one's life on a possibility. When the Hebrews said, "In the beginning God," they were affirming their willingness to risk that there was meaning behind the universe, that we were not just creatures cast mindlessly into the void. There is purpose to creation. None of this can be proved. All efforts to prove God, I believe, are evidence of the hubris of the creature. Our response can only be to risk that there is a God or that there is not. Biblical faith risks that there is.

Biblical faith goes on to assert that God created the world. God is the explanation for all that is. We often get so troubled by the powerful presence of evil in our world that we are tempted to go the way of other religions and set up two Gods, the god of darkness and the god of light. Biblical faith struggles on the exciting journey from monolatry—"thou shalt have no other Gods before me" (Exodus 20:3)—to monotheism— "To whom then will ye liken me, or shall I be equal? saith the Holy One" (Isaiah 40:25). There is one God, and that one God is a creator. Creation is an act of love. The most important thing that Biblical faith says about God is that God is a lover. That is a daring assertion. Other faiths posit a warrior God. (Sometimes we wistfully slip into that formula, too.) Other faiths posit a detached Being above the struggle. (That idea also has its attraction for us.) But Biblical faith risks a God as a Lover. A lover is always vulnerable to the beloved. A vulnerable God. What a vision!

The third affirmation in that first sentence is that the world was created good. God's work was good. God's intent was that the world be good. The world started off good—"A friendly world of friendly folk beneath a friendly sky," as Howard Thurman phrased it. Biblical faith holds that creation has fallen. Creation is not as God intended it to be.

The Second Sentence: The free creatures in that creation rejected living under the rule of God and set in motion the drama of God's reconciliation. God, the lover, offered human beings, the beloved, the possibility of life under the rule of God; but God could only offer it. The lover is always vulnerable to the beloved. The lover can always say no. Love is only love if freely given. The beloved always has a choice. The Biblical Story has it that God gave the human creatures everything—a beautiful environment, plenty of food to eat, satisfying work to do, companionship, and a relationship with God. The relationship, however, was not one of equals. God could set the parameters. "Of every tree of the garden thou mayest freely eat: But of the tree of the knowledge of good and evil, thou shalt not eat of it" (Genesis 2:16b–17a). The relationship should be one of creator to creature, God to the subordinate being. That was the contract that was rejected. The temptation was to be as gods. We call the moment of succumbing to that temptation the Fall, the exercise of human freedom to go another way than the way God had planned. Biblical faith is that God did not give up on God's dream. The rest of the Biblical Story is the Story of God's working to reconcile God's free creatures to the creator.

The Third Sentence: The drama began in the Old Testament with God's choosing a people, the Hebrews, to live out before the world God's way. The Story ranges over universal history—Cain and Abel, Noah and the flood, the tower of Babel—before it settles down to one people, the calling of Abraham. "Get thee out of thy country, and from thy kindred, and from thy father's house, unto a land that I will show thee . . . and in thee shall all families of the earth be blessed" (Genesis 12:1b,3b). Something new was happening in the world. Every past relationship and understanding was to be abandoned. God was about to do a new thing, and God was about to do it for all the peoples of the world. Election and chosenness in the Bible is always election and chosenness for God's purposes, and God's purpose is always to restore the fallen creation. God does not give up because creation is fallen. God works to bring in the New Creation, and God calls on the human creatures to work with God. Biblical faith has the amazing understanding that the Omnipotent wills to limit omnipotence. The Biblical God is one whose strength is made perfect in weakness. And so this God calls a people to live out God's dream before the world. God keeps the cultic memory of a promise to an ancestor through all the tribulations of migrations, famine, slavery, deliverance, the wilderness experience of uniqueness and covenant, and nationhood. The possibility was to be the new thing in the world, but the chosen people chose to be like all the other nations in the world. The ever-patient God—how impatient we get with the terrible patience of God!—did not abandon them but sent the prophets to recall them to their mission.

The Fourth Sentence: The drama climaxes in the New Testament with God's entering history to be God's Way incarnate. Jesus came to turn the existing order upside down and to declare that the acceptable year of the Lord is here. His life was guided by commitment to one absolute—God. That commitment made him a threat to religious and political authorities. He gathered around him the nucleus of a people of God which would include as diverse a group of people as you can imagine. He lived out with them a model of lordship which scandalized all their understandings. The master would wash the feet of his disciples, and the Messiah would suffer and die. On the third day they saw that God's way was the Way, and in resurrection power they set out to change the world and restore it to what God wanted it to be.

The Fifth Sentence: The drama continues beyond the pages of the Bible with the people of God, the Christian Church called to be the continuing agent of God's reconciling work. God's work is not done. We in the Christian Church are called to be a part of that work. That ongoing work of God—restoring the fallen creation—is, I think, what Jesus taught us to pray about: "Thy kingdom come. They will be done on earth as it is in heaven." "Thy will be done *on earth.*" I think we can understand God's will only as we know the total Biblical Story. I think the people of God, the Christian Church, will only know that Story as they are called to reflect on it week after week in the drama of the liturgy and the words of the sermon. All who preach, I think, must know that total Story, must be able to tell it, and must preach always with the total Story in mind.

How Can We Preach the Story? What does it mean to preach with the total Story in mind on any given Sunday? For the sake of example, I will choose the Fourth Sunday of Advent, Year A. The Propers for this Sunday are:

Isaiah 7:10–17

Psalm 24 or 24:1–7

Romans 1:1–17

Matthew 1:18–25

The preparation for a sermon should always begin, in my opinion, with a sound exegesis of the Scripture passages offered by the lectionary. In this initial work of familiarizing ourselves with these readings, an important question to keep in mind is "What was going on in the life of the people at the time this passage reflects?" In other words, what is the history out of which it came? In our study of the Scriptures we rush prematurely to "What does the passage say to me?" I do not think we really can have any sound idea of what it says to us before we know what it said to the people who thought it was important enough to preserve it. Biblical faith holds that God uses the canvas of history to reveal God's great design.

Not paying sufficient attention to history has fostered the perception of prophets as prognosticators foretelling the future instead of the "speakers for God" (as their name means) who hold up the past commitments against the present betrayals of those commitments. Prophets make us very uncomfortable, just as in the first reading for the Fourth Sunday in Advent for Year A, Isaiah is making Ahaz very uncomfortable. Ahaz is in a tight place, besieged by threatening armies on either side, and he is frantically looking for help from strong neighbors. He does not want to hear from the counsellor who advises the age-old faith, "Trust in God!" Isaiah offers a sign. With false piety Ahaz declares that he will not tempt God. Isaiah gives him the sign anyway. There is a young woman at court who is going to have a child who will be named Emmanuel—God with us; and before that child is many years old, you will know that God is with God's people because the allies you think so strong will witness the continuation of the Davidic monarchy against all odds.

The psalm acts as a great Amen to the Old Testament lesson. From an Old Testament lesson that reminds us God is in control, we join in an expression of worship that is a response to that kind of God: "The earth is the Lord's and all that is in it, the world and all who dwell therein."

Following the Story, the Gospel passage must be considered next. On this Sunday just before Christmas, we have the Matthean account of the birth of Jesus. The early Christians were ever eager to affirm that they were in the line of God's Story from the beginning. They were not some strange new deviation, some distortion of the tradition. They were the natural evolution of God's great plan. One of the ways Matthew affirms this continuity is to identify significant events with a prooftext. "And now all this was done," says Matthew, "That it might be fulfilled which was spoken of the Lord by the prophet . . ."

What did the early Church make of the dialogue between the Old and New Testaments we hear in these Scriptures? The Epistle suggests one answer to that question. On this particular Sunday, St. Paul is looked to for the connection: the first seven verses of St. Paul's Letter to the Romans. Paul is preeminently the one to do this because he had to answer that question for himself. How did a distinguished exemplar of the faith, a Pharisee of the Pharisees, become a member of a community he had bitterly persecuted as apostate? What did he see that he hadn't seen before? There was that desert period when he obviously wrestled through to his answer, but he so quickly plunged into his work of evangelization and of being the chief support system for the little congregations he had called into being, that he had had little time to write out a closely reasoned statement of his understanding. Then came the possibility of going to Rome. It was a significant church in the capital city of the empire. These people did not know Paul, except perhaps by reputation, and that knowledge was not always favorable. Paul had to present himself to them. Paul had to spell out his understanding of God's action from the creation of the world. The opening sentences of his Letter to the Romans, which the lectionary offers as the Epistle for this Sunday, are really one long sentence. Paul focuses on Jesus as the climactic act of God and uses phrases that may have been developing creedal statements among the early Christians: the Son descended from David according to the flesh, designated Son of God according to the Spirit by his resurrection from the dead.

Having done the exegesis, the next step in sermon preparation is to wait on the Scriptures until a theme from the Story emerges for you from these Scriptures.

In listening for a theme, keep in mind that many different sermons can come from the same Scriptures. There is no one right sermon. The sermon is the response of the preacher to the Scriptures. This is the point at which the preacher wrestles with the question often asked prematurely, "What does the Scripture say to me?" After having done the study and meditation that are the prerequisites for careful discernment, the preacher offers in the sermon what the preacher believes to be a faithful response to that question.

Remember your summary of the Story as you listen for a theme to emerge from the Scripture for the day. On the Fourth Sunday of Advent we are about to celebrate the climax of God's action to reconcile the world unto God. The Old Testament lesson reminds

THE RECALLING OF THE SACRED STORY

us that God is ever active in the events of history. God is not an indifferent or a powerless bystander. The psalm celebrates God's power. The Gospel affirms God's entrance into history. The Epistle reminds us of the response of the community of faith, the people of God, to that entrance into history. A theme emerges: God working in the events of history.

The theme can often be further focused by considering where we are in the liturgical year. After the Fourth Sunday of Advent, the next time the worshipping community gathers is for the celebration of the Christmas Feast. The Collect for the day calls us to attend to God's daily visitation. The sermon on this last Sunday in Advent will prepare the community for the great visitation which is the climax of the sacred Story: God with us, Emmanuel.

Now it is possible to sketch the movement of the sermon:

The story began with the creation of a good world by a loving God. The free creatures in that creation rejected living in accordance with God's dream. God did not abandon the creation but is ever present in it to reconcile the creature to the creator. We need eyes to see. We need eyes to see in the daily routines of our lives the being of God pressing upon us. We need the prophetic faith and vision of God's chosen ones who speak for God in order to see—even as we read the daily newspapers—how God is working God's purpose out. Even as Isaiah did, we need the courage to speak to the rulers of the kingdoms of the world concerning the other possibility offered by the Kingdom of God. We need to see in a little baby born to a peasant woman the culmination of God's plan for the restoring of the fallen creation. We need to see in the life, death, and resurrection of that Baby another Way for the fallen creation. We need to take our place in that glorious company of those called to be saints, the Christian Church, and to heed the call to us to be a part of God's continuing work of reconciliation.

This would be one possibility for recalling the sacred Story in the sermon for this day. No sermon exhausts the possibilities of how the Story is reflected in the given Scriptures. The sermon, ideally, is an invitation to dialogue. "Here is how I saw it," says the preacher. "How did you see it?" I believe every sermon should be followed by a response from the community as we share how our story participates in the Story and interacts, under the stimulus of the Scriptures for the day, with the stories of other members of the people of God. In this way we can be reminded that the reconciling work of God goes on and on, and that we too have a part in the Story.

Preaching through

The Church Year

Advent

Louis Weil

THE PRIMARY CHALLENGE a preacher encounters during Advent is the complexity of the season itself. There is, in the first place, the extraordinary richness of the images and themes found in the cycle of biblical readings, including substantial reference to the powerful figure of John the Baptist as well as to the dramatic events associated with the Annunciation and the Incarnation. In addition to that, the Advent season carries a heavy weight of historical baggage coming out of the factors which shaped its evolution within the Church Year, especially the persistence of a penitential aspect to the season which has the effect of keeping Advent in some places as a kind of quasi-Lent.

There is also the grave difficulty which the season encounters in reference to the larger social context in our culture as the Church celebrates rites related to the coming of Christ, either in preparation for the commemoration of his birth in history on the feast of Christmas, or in looking forward to his coming at the end of human history, while our culture as a whole is caught up in the generally secular events derived from the Christmas event. When the Church arrives at the actual celebration of the birth of Jesus, our society is already exhausted with its routine and weary of the theme and its musical accompaniment. The dissonance which the practicing Christian encounters in this social dislocation needs to be taken seriously since the impact of the larger cultural context often shapes the churchgoer's experience of the pre-Christmas season more forcefully than the liturgical celebrations of the four Sundays of Advent could ever hope to do. For preachers, all of these factors must be kept in mind as we prepare what we want to proclaim in our liturgical homilies during the Advent season.

Historical Perspectives on Advent

Advent first emerged in the context of Western Christian society. Similar to Easter with its period of preparation, the birth of Jesus came to be preceded by a period of weeks which focused on the Church's anticipation of his coming, and which thus took the name of Advent (from the Latin *adventus*, coming or arrival). The first evidence available to us cf a season of preparation for Christmas is found in Spain. Strictly speaking, this early evidence is related to the preparation for the celebration of baptism on the feast of the Epiphany on January 6, rather than to liturgies of Advent as such.

In Gaul, there was an eight-week period known as "St. Martin's Lent" which lasted from the feast of St. Martin (November 11) to the Epiphany. Within that fifty-six day period, there were forty days designated for fasting. The focus of this fast was baptism on the feast of the Epiphany, so that the baptisms on that date might be accorded the same intensity of preparation as were the baptisms at Easter with their preparatory fasts during the season of Lent. We do not know how widely this custom was observed, but we do have evidence for it in northern Europe.

The first evidence for an actual liturgy of Advent is found in northern Italy in the mid-fifth century. The primary theme of this early evidence is expectation for the birth of Jesus. By the end of the sixth century, we find in the sacramentary organized by Gregory the Great at Rome the provision of four sets of eucharistic propers for the four Sundays prior to Christmas, the pattern which

Advent was to take within the formalized structure of the calendar. The focus for these four Sundays is the Incarnation of Jesus Christ and the Church's preparation for its celebration.

In northern Europe, on the other hand, another emphasis emerged within the Advent cycle, namely, the eschatological dimension, the expectation for the final return of the Lord as judge at the end of time. It is in this context that a penitential theme came to be attached to Advent. Under the influence of the preaching of Irish monastics such as Columbanus (530–615), a strong emphasis was placed upon the need to do penance before the final judgment which would occur when the Lord returned. This penitential approach to Advent led, in the Gallican rites, to the dropping of the Alleluia from the eucharist in Advent, and to the use of purple vestments. For yet another reason, not in regard to baptismal preparation but in regard to a penitential emphasis, Advent was coming to be seen as a kind of second Lent.

This penitential character was slow in moving south to Rome, but by the twelfth century, purple vesture had come to be associated with the Roman rite in Advent. The Alleluia, however, was retained, indicating a typical Roman reserve toward this innovation in the Gallican rites. The Roman pattern of four Sundays eventually dominated as the length of Advent, although a period of up to six weeks was kept in some dioceses, and this practice has continued to the present in the rite of Milan.

The association of eschatological images with the season of Advent is the result of a gradual narrowing of those images in the Church Year from what was, for Christians of the first centuries, a fundamental aspect of all Christian liturgical celebrations. In both I Corinthians and the Didache, the use of the exclamation *Maranatha* points to an eschatological understanding of the Church's worship. The word carries a double meaning, "our Lord has come" or "our Lord, come," but in either case the relation of the liturgy to the coming of Christ is clear. In the worship of the earliest Christian communities, there seems to have been a vivid awareness that the risen Lord was present among them, and that the liturgy somehow offered a privileged experience of his presence. From the fourth century onward, this eschatological sense diminished, but in the eventual emergence of the season of Advent some hint of it was preserved by being linked to the Christmas-Epiphany cycle with its focus upon the Incarnation of the Lord.

Recent liturgical writing has called for a recovery of this eschatological perspective. It is reflected in the increased use of such images in the new eucharistic prayers of the 1979 Book of Common Prayer:

Eucharistic Prayer A:". . . at the last day bring us with all your saints into the joy of your eternal kingdom."

Eucharistic Prayer B:"In the fullness of time, put all things in subjection under your Christ . . ."

Eucharistic Prayer C:"We celebrate his death and resurrection, as we await the day of his coming."

Eucharistic Prayer D:". . . proclaiming his resurrection and ascension to your right hand, awaiting his coming in glory . . ." This forward-looking dimension is a recovery of an aspect of liturgical prayer which was virtually absent from the past-oriented rites used by the Church prior to recent reforms.

In the Church Year, this emphasis can be seen particularly in the final phase of the weeks after Pentecost, culminating in the feast of Christ the King as an image of the final consummation. That feast marks the threshold of Advent which, especially on its first Sunday, speaks of the final judgment and our need to be prepared. In this context, Advent points the Church in two directions, backward to the coming of Jesus in history in the humility of his birth, and forward toward the awaited coming of Christ at the end of time as the One who brings history to its fulfillment.

The Advent Cycle of Readings

Episcopalians who remember the annual cycle of readings retained through the 1928 BCP will perhaps associate the beginning of the Advent season with the reading of Matthew 21:1–13, the recounting of the triumphal entry of Jesus into Jerusalem. The events described in that reading are, of course, directly connected to the days prior to the crucifixion and are thus more appropriate to their association with Palm Sunday and the Church's reenactment of the procession. Although the reading from Matthew 21 has now been removed from the Advent readings, it is a helpful reminder of the multilayered dimensions of Advent in its relating of an eschatological image of the appearance of Christ hailed as ruler by his people with the season of commemoration of his birth in human history. This multilayered aspect of Advent has been enhanced by a three-year lectionary which offers the Church a more extensive view of Advent images, and thus gives the preacher an opportunity for a more concentrated focus on any given Sunday within the three-year cycle.

On the first Sunday of Advent, the gospel readings speak of the return of the Lord and call for watchfulness as a response. This emphasis upon the second coming of Christ is supported by the readings appointed from the Old Testament from Isaiah (2:1–5, in year A, and 64:1–9a, in year B) and Zechariah (14:4–9, in year C). These readings speak of the coming of the Messiah to judge the world and to bring the final days to an end. The New Testament readings are taken from various letters of Paul and express themes which form an interesting counterpoint to the eschatological images of the first reading and the gospel. In year A, Paul warns that we must "cast off the works of darkness" because "the day is at hand" (Romans 13:8–14). The appointed reading for year B is both a greeting and an expression of thankfulness to God for the gifts given to those whom Paul is addressing, who "wait for the revealing of our Lord Jesus Christ; who will sustain you to the end, guiltless in the day of our Lord Jesus Christ" (I Corinthians 1:1–9). Finally, in year C, Paul calls for his hearers to grow in love for one another and toward all people, so that the Lord "may establish your hearts unblamable in holiness before our God and Father, at the coming of our Lord Jesus Christ with all his saints" (I Thessalonians 3:9–13).

For the preacher, the challenge as the season of Advent is initiated on this first Sunday is to recognize the multiplicity of images which are offered by the appointed readings. They invite the preacher to draw forth complementary images from personal experience, and from the life of the community or the wider society, in which the relation between how we live daily is seen in the context of our recognition of Christ's presence breaking into our lives. That is the fundamental theme of Advent: the coming of the Lord. But it is a theme which elicits a wide range of expression since the Lord who has come in history and who will come to bring that history to its fulfillment is also the One who is present with us here and now, the One "with whom we have to do."

However the preacher may have set this context on the first Sunday of Advent, the following three Sundays offer the occasions to relate this theme of the coming of the Lord to two powerful human symbols of preparation: John the Baptist and the Blessed Virgin Mary. John dominates the second and third Sundays of Advent; for the fourth, at the gateway to Christmas, the Church turns its attention to the birth of Jesus and thus inevitably to Mary as mother of the Lord.

The gospel readings appointed for Advent II in the three-year cycle are all concerned with the first appearance of John the Baptist and his call to repentance. Once again, about as often as we can stand it, that strange, passionate man, dressed in crude clothing and munching on insects, stands before us. He offers a marvelous disjuncture from the decency and order which generally characterize Anglican worship, and his message is no more appealing than his strange dress: "Repent." And for those of his hearers actively involved in religious matters, John's language is even stronger:

> You brood of vipers! Who warned you to flee from the wrath to come? (Matthew 3:7)

We must not in our preaching tame John the Baptist: his passion is integral to his message. The Church needs still to hear him with all the disturbing impact of his words. We must not ignore John since he stands so firmly within the context of the narrative of the saving events accomplished by Jesus. The challenge for the preacher is to relate this strange man to ourselves today. He seems remote, a weird figure criticizing a religious system from which we feel profoundly removed. At the heart of John's message, however, there is a prophetic word as imperative to our time as to any. It is a proclamation of God's light in a darkened world: as the Fourth Gospel tells us, "he came to bear witness to the light." To accomplish this, John spoke forcefully and passionately to his hearers, and, through the preacher, can speak to us, so that their hearts and ours might be penetrated by God's entry into our lives. For those of us who seek to express our faith in daily living, John's word is urgent: do not be complacent about your relation with God for "God is able from these stones to raise up children to Abraham."

On the third Sunday of Advent, we see John's ministry brought to term as he gives way to the arrival of Jesus on the scene. His work wanes as that of Jesus is undertaken. For this Sunday, as for Advent II, the image of John is central, but on Advent III attention is given to John as he speaks of him "who is to come." Yet even in this context Jesus says of him, "among those born of women there has risen no one greater than John the Baptist" (Matthew 11:2,11, in year A). The ancillary character of John's ministry is indicated in both of two optional gospel readings in year B: "I baptize with water; but among you stands one whom you do not know, even he who comes after me, the thong of whose sandal I am not worthy to untie" (John 1:6–8, 19–28), and in the alternative readings, "I am not the Christ, but I have been sent before him. . . . He must increase, but I must decrease" (John 3:23–30). In cycle C, the gospel reading includes both John's moral challenge to his hearers as well as his reference to the coming Christ "who is mightier than I . . . the thong of whose sandal I am not worthy to untie," and thus parallels the material from Matthew appointed for Advent III in cycle A.

The emphasis upon John the Baptist on Advent II and III as the precursor of the Lord sets the context for the realization of that coming in the Incarnation and in the birth which Christmas celebrates. Advent IV turns the Church's attention to God's initiative in the saving events as recorded in the angel's announcements to Joseph about Mary (in cycle A) and directly to Mary (in cycle B), and even more pointedly upon Mary herself for her blessedness as mother of the incarnate Lord (in cycle C). Regardless of the appointed Gospel in any given year, there is an assumed familiarity with the Lukan account of the Annunciation (Luke 1:26–38), which invariably appears in the lectionary for the celebration of that feast on March 25.

Given the content of the gospel readings appointed for Advent IV in the three-year cycle, it is difficult to imagine preaching on this day without giving some attention to Mary and her role in salvation history. This is, however, not a comfortable task in the Episcopal Church if we may judge from the infrequency with which such preaching takes place. The problem is that devotion to Mary, or even special attention to her, evokes for many people an anxiety over an excessive attention to Mary which has characterized Roman Catholic piety. For Anglicans, Cranmer's reference to Jesus as "our only Mediator and Advocate" has taken deep root within our spirituality. Although there is significant consideration of Mary among Anglican writers of the last four centuries, on the whole little attention is given to her in our popular piety, except for references in Christmas hymns and carols. Because of Mary's indisputable place in the story of the birth of Jesus, such references are acceptable even to people for whom attention to Mary would be viewed as discordant with Anglican piety.

Mary's role in the birth of Jesus is the fundamental source of her significance for Christians. This view is confirmed when we learn that the earliest commemoration of Mary in the western Christian calendar was on January 1, and it was as a celebration of her motherhood. In other words, the attention to Mary suggested by the gospel readings assigned to the three-year cycle for Advent IV connects directly to an early Christian insight concerning the Lord's mother as the human instrument of the Incarnation.

Given the incarnational orientation of both Anglican theology and spirituality, it would seem fitting that at least on the annual occasion offered by the lectionary for Advent IV, the preacher should attempt to present a theologically balanced understanding of Mary's place in Christian piety, seeing her as an example of one who accepted God's will for her even in very confusing circumstances, and who remained faithful. Mary is thus an abiding example to Christians that all of us, as we are obedient to God, can become instruments of God's presence and activity in the world. In that perspective, it is evident why "all generations will call [her] blessed." Preaching on Advent IV offers a challenge neither to focus upon Mary in herself, nor, in reaction, to ignore her, but rather to recognize in her role as mother of the Lord a sign to all Christians of God's exaltation of the lowly who offer their lives in faith and obedience.

The Conflict of Advent with our Culture

Whereas the preacher may attentively develop these themes of expectation and fulfillment which are lifted up in the lectionary of Advent through a variety of images, the people who assemble on its four Sundays are living most of the hours of their lives in a world which is dancing to a very different tune. Once Thanksgiving has passed, if not earlier, the business world has convinced us that Christmas has already arrived, and social patterns have responded to that program by turning December into a month of Christmas celebrations which so exhaust us with their demands that Christmas day becomes a blessed end to a tiring round of obligations. If preachers are not realistic about this social reality, the tendency to see the liturgy as encapsulated in its own world of images and disconnected from the real world can only be intensified. The Church already suffers from a generally schizoid understanding of liturgy in which one can say or sing just about anything without fearing that it will connect with choices in our real lives. What our society is engaged in during the month of December makes the risk of this disjuncture all the greater in the season of Advent.

How can the preacher address what the pre-Christmas season has become through the impact of not only the aims of the business world but, more significantly, of that within ourselves for which commercialization is but the response of supply to demand, the idea that the meaning of life is found in the acquisition of things? How do we preach to that social reality without sounding simply negative and joyless and thus confirming the disjuncture with our society's appropriate need to celebrate? How do we preach in a society where gift-giving often becomes tit-for-tat without obscuring that in our relation to God all is gift, that

Christmas is itself preeminently a celebration of God's gift, and that the gift does elicit a response, the response of praise?

The challenges to the preacher are formidable, but the season of Advent itself offers perhaps the best path by which to penetrate our society's pattern in the hope of transforming it in the light of the Gospel. Advent recognizes our incompleteness and proclaims that it is only God's gift which can fill that hole. Deep within ourselves, we discern at times the vanity of mere acquisition; we recognize that the hole remains no matter how many things we acquire. Advent suggests that our gifts which spring from love are a kind of reverberation of the great gift, God's self-disclosure in Jesus, and that only that gift, which comes to us in a dazzling humility, can fulfill the expectation which the season proclaims.

Christmas

Herbert O'Driscoll

THE PROSPECT OF PREACHING the good news of our Lord Jesus Christ at the season of his birth is one full of ironies. On the one hand there is no searching for a theme for our homilies. It shines in front of us, obvious, unavoidable, beckoning. The scriptures we are offered are endlessly rich with possibilities. The message at the heart of it all, that of birth—more, that of Incarnation, the birthing of God in the world—is perhaps the deepest longing in every human being within reach of the homilist's voice. Is there any reason then why preaching in this season can be other than privilege and joy?

The Demons of the Season

Yes, there is. While one would hope that the preacher will always deem it a privilege (if we no longer do so, we should do some serious self-examination), there are good reasons why Christmas homilizing is not always a joy. Perhaps it would be more accurate to say that the prospect of preaching at Christmas is often less than a joy. Strangely enough the actual occasion of our preaching is almost always itself lifted to joy by the mysterious power of the season. But certain realities remain. First, there is usually a good deal of all-too-human agenda going on in the preacher's own life. There is probably too much socializing to be done as well-meaning friends and parishioners heap invitations on us. Family may be arriving or already arrived. There have probably been special events in the parish's life. One may be aware of certain people who have been bereaved since last Christmas, and perhaps there have been some contacts made. Because of the intensity of the season, there may be pastoral demands affecting marriages, relationships with children, or the loneliness of those who quite simply and unavoidably are alone. We do not need many years of experience in priesthood to realize the demons which this season can unbind in human awareness. It is not for nothing that W. B. Yeats speaks of a dark beast slouching toward Bethlehem even as a gentler and more malleable beast bears his sacred burden to the waiting stable. All of the above factors, to name only some, serve to ensure that the homilist can come to the task of preaching feeling very much an earthen vessel.

There are less earthy but no less forbidding elements present here. Above all these is the strange paradox that all preachers feel when they are confronted by the great and high seasons of the faith. On the one hand everyone knows what is to be told. Everyone comes and kneels and prays and sings precisely because they know the story. This story has drawn people here like a powerful magnet. There is not a soul, young or old, who does not know why this is a "Silent night, holy night." In the same way there will come a Sunday in the Spring when every soul, young or old, will know that "Jesus Christ is risen today." We may question the depth of such knowing, and such a questioning is quite valid, but the reality remains that on such high feast days the great overriding facts of the feast itself are known. What then can possibly be said that is even remotely fresh? What can be formed on the tantalizingly blank page beneath our study light that has any hope of grasping the mind and the heart of those who will be there in front of us? Such can be the feelings and fears which can overwhelm the preparing of a Christmas homily.

The Angels of the Season

Thank God, such feelings and fears can be challenged. The preacher might begin with a self-reminder that this story has drawn here not only those who regularly worship but also many who have slight acquaintance with the Church and the faith it represents, yet who nevertheless feel a mysterious pull to these lights, this music, this story told again and again and again. Knowing this, the preacher should realize some things which can be of enormous encouragement when preparing to preach.

The first is that the story itself, the event itself, possesses immense power. It is about something that every listener longs to hear in his or her deepest being. The second thing is that on the actual eve of Christmas and on the day itself the gates of the human spirit are opened in a way we seldom find them. There is something about this season that pierces through all our carefully constructed rationality, control, dominance. The Christ child is more powerful than all of these things. He summons out to meet him the child within all of us. If for no other reason than this, the preacher preparing a homily would be wise not to worship at the altar of rationality, analysis, explanation. Instead there will be a searching for poetry, imagination, mystery. Michael Ramsey, at one time Archbishop of Canterbury, said that there is in the Gospel both Story and Glory. The story can be told to a child; the glory is so deep and full of wonder that the greatest human intellect cannot exhaust it. As the preacher goes to give the homily on this "holy night," all the wonder of the simple story is only waiting to be released to do battle with the world-weariness, the hurts, and the cynicism which form an armor of resistance about so much modern life. Something of this must have been in the mind of Phillips Brooks when he wrote of Bethlehem that "the hopes and fears of all the years are met in thee tonight." In a mysterious way this is true also of the Bethlehem which is every human heart in the congregation. Hopes and fears meet, mingling and clashing— not to mention all the years of memory in older lives and of anticipation in the young.

About Preparation

Long before the eve of Christmas the preacher's preparation should begin. This is true of all the great Christian feasts. Such seasons, and most of all, Christmas and Easter, are anything but ordinary times. In the deepest and loveliest sense of the word they are mysteries. A mystery, let us remember, is not something we can know nothing about. A mystery is that which is so multi-levelled and so many-splendored that no amount of examination and reflection can exhaust its meaning.

Because Christmas is such a time, the preacher needs to prepare for the task of preaching its meaning. That preparation needs to begin at least as soon as the first store or the first advertisement or the first radio jingle signals that Christmas is only X number of shopping days away. Nowadays that time can come when one is liturgically still in All Saints! Instead of railing against this as secular commercialism (which it certainly is), we can use it as a call to open a file for the Christmas homily. I mean this quite literally. Anything that occurs to the mind about our Lord's Incarnation from this time on should go into that file. The small human incident, the casual remark, the paragraph stumbled upon, the new slant on familiar scripture that occurs to one, the magazine article, the seemingly disconnected thought. When the time comes to open this file not everything in it will be found useful, but it will be a great gift not to be starting from scratch.

The Themes within the Season

To preach at Christmas in the final years of this century is to have an opportunity of announcing certain themes that resonate in the human spirit. We know we are preaching the mystery we call Incarnation, but let us consider the endless ramifications of this. Incarnation is a many-faceted diamond. To preach it means speaking of birth, hope, new life, new beginning, fulfillment, the future, the struggle for all these things, the cost of bringing them to birth, the meaning of the child in each of us, the paradoxical ways of God in the world. This is still a far from complete list. As the images and cadences of the story sound for us again, each of us as preachers will find new faces of the timeless diamond of Incarnation shining for us and inviting our reflection.

Every preacher will decide in what way and with what emphases to direct these themes. Will the Incarnation of our Lord be spoken of as a grace given to us to make us aware of these things in our contemporary personal experience, or will it be spoken of as grace given to us to discern them in society and the life of the nation or the world? Are these themes at all discernible in one's own personal experience, in one's profession, in one's marriage, in one's relationships with one's children? Where are these themes present in the life of today's church? Where are they present in the policies of our nation? Where and how can they be expressed as present in our ongoing struggle towards awareness of and response to environmental challenges? The possibilities for application range across the whole spectrum of human experience, from the human heart to the cosmos itself.

The Scriptures of the Season

If such a range is possible, what of the instruments given to the preacher to accomplish this task? What of the scriptures the preacher has to hand? They too range from the intimate and personal to the infinite and the cosmic. They are lyrical. They sing rather than speak. To use a phrase of Kipling, they "splash at a ten league canvas with a brush of comet's hair." Their first voice is that of a man whose vision was nothing less than planetary, for whom nations were no more than drops on the edge of a bucket before the throne of God. We know him as Isaiah. The second voice, that of Paul, has not uttered a dozen words before it encompasses the whole of humanity within this event. Even Luke begins with a vista of empire and ultimate earthly power before exchanging this panorama for the intimacy and vulnerability of the young couple moving toward their rendezvous with birth. Then, as if unable to stay with such a close lens, Luke sweeps us among the galaxies as soon as the crying child lies glistening on the blood-stained straw. He too joins the other voices of scripture. Like them he is unable to use anything less than all of time, all of humanity, and all of creation as the backdrop to this event. Finally, as if he is afraid that such cosmic imagery will remove the significance of the birth from those of us who must live out the reality of daily human experience, Luke assails our nostrils and ears with the utterly earthy world of the shepherds' field!

The Voice of Isaiah   (Isaiah 9:2–4,6–7)

To say that *people walk in darkness* is a description of contemporary reality. We inhabit a wintertime of history, both in the body politic and in the human soul. Such a time longs for the images of light. What is significant about this light is that it blazes in the unexpected place and in an unexpected time. That is terribly important, for only if we have learned to look in the unexpected place, only if we have come to know that this is God's paradoxical way, do we have a chance of seeing light in our own experience and in our own time. To say that *unto us a child is born* is to speak to the deep threat to the whole of humanity which is at the heart of contemporary reality. When we add that this child is not just any child, when we name him *Prince of Peace*, we speak with power to a culture always aware of the possibility of armed conflict beyond our capacity to imagine. As Christians we are prepared to go farther. We name the child *son* and we mean *Son of God*. We are claiming nothing less than the entry of divinity onto the stage of humanity, of eternity onto the stage of time. We are claiming that the author of the human story, indeed of the story of the whole creation, has walked on stage.

The Voice of the Psalmist   (Psalm 96)

Once again we are swept immediately to the universal. The *new song* of this night is for *the whole earth*. There follows an ecstatic song about God, a lyrical celebration of God's attributes and God's preeminence. The psalm probes the earth from end to end. *All nations* are involved. All of humanity is seen within the totality of creation. *The sea, the field, all the trees of the wood*, all are *glad:* they *thunder*, they are *joyful*, they *shout for joy*. The reality of God affects humanity, history, nature.

The Voice of Paul   (Titus 2:11–14)

Suddenly we hear pen on paper writing a letter. The letter makes a claim: *the grace of God has appeared for the salvation of all.* The keystone of this statement is the word *all.* Whatever has happened in this solitary woman's womb has happened in the womb of the whole world, in the womb of all time. That is the true reason why this giving of birth is like none other. However difficult an increasingly plural world makes the expression of this, nothing less than this expresses Christian faith. If it be true that God encounters our humanity in this birth, then our humanity has been given new meaning. What has in fact happened to us is that we have been called to new responsibility. We are called to the immensely liberating realization that we are not helpless in the face of history. We can act. We can be a people *zealous for good deeds.*

The Voice of Luke   (Luke 2:1–20)

There is immediately a fascinating set of contrasts in what Luke tells us. He starts out on a vast scale. We are at the heart of absolute power in the world of that time. The emperor is making a decision that is going to affect the lives of every man, woman, and child in the empire. The machinery of the census begins to roll across the world. Now Luke puts a succession of decreasing lenses on his camera as he takes us across the empire. We move from Rome to Syria. Here is the emperor's delegated power. Now we are in the village of Nazareth in the province of Galilee. Here there is no power. There is just an ordinary man named Joseph. He doesn't make world-shaking decisions. He has to respond to them. We have moved from power to powerlessness.

But have we? Notice how in verse 4 we refer to a long-ago center of power, long before Rome. We hear the name of David, King in Israel. Is Luke subtly saying that there is another kind of power involved in what is happening, older, less obvious, more mysterious? Perhaps if we are prepared to look very closely and to probe the ways of God we will see what this power really is.

So far Luke has given us an emperor and a newborn child. Could there be a greater contrast in terms of power and vulnerability? But wait. We should look again. This is God at work, therefore we should examine very carefully things as they appear to be. With God appearances can be deceptive. We are told again and again in the Bible that God's ways are not our ways. We need to be told this truth again and again because we consistently forget it.

God does not work with the things or the people or the circumstances or the resources that may seem so right and so desirable to us. Rome is vast and powerful. Bethlehem is a pathetic village. But it is in Bethlehem where timeless glory is encountered. Caesar is mighty and, in comparison, Joseph is weak, even helpless; yet to Joseph is given the incomparable privilege of caring for the child of God. Mary is an unknown villager, yet she is the instrument through whom a reality almost beyond words comes into being. As with Joseph, as with Mary, so with each of us. We are ordinary and all too human; yet the eternal God is prepared to use us, such as we are, in the formation of today's world, not to mention tomorrow's.

The Vision of the Creche

Nothing shows us more clearly the cosmic dimension of this season than to gaze into a creche, no matter how splendid or how primitive it may be. It can be inexpensive and tiny, sitting on top of the TV in a one-room apartment. It can be massive and elaborate outside a cathedral in a thundering city. What do we see? At the center of it lies the child. The child is everything. The child is possibility, birth, new humanity, tomorrow. The child is the instrument of God to fashion all that is to be. Look on either side of the child. Behold the man and the woman. In them both are two human mysteries, femininity and masculinity. Both are necessary for the working of God. Both are needed to form the future being. Look beyond these two. There stand two groups, shepherds and magi, again symbolizing two aspects of our humanity, hand and mind. Beyond and among them we see the animals, companion life forms in creation. Above them all gleams the star. All the interwoven tapestry of creation is here in this deceptively simple creche. All is interconnected, together forming an ecology of creation. The creche is in effect a miniature planet. Nor does seeing the symbols of this season through such a mythic lens diminish by one iota their particular and specific significance for Christian faith.

That specific significance of the Incarnation has never been more simply and beautifully expressed than in the lines of John Betjeman, that devout and faithful churchman, once poet laureate of England, who has written in his ballad entitled "Christmas":

And is it true? And is it true,
This most tremendous tale of all,
Seen in a stained glass window's hue,
A baby in an ox's stall?
The Maker of the stars and sea
Become a Child on earth for me?

No love that in a family dwells,
No carolling in frosty air,
Nor all the steeple-shaking bells
Can with this single truth compare—
That God was Man in Palestine
And lives today in Bread and Wine.

One is tempted to say that if a preacher did no more than quote these lovely and gentle lines, the Good News of God in Christ would have been preached more than adequately.

Epiphany Season

Reginald H. Fuller

Introduction: Understanding the Shape of the Season

The three-year lectionary as originally designed for the Roman Catholic Church had no Epiphany season. January 6th was retained as the traditional Western Epiphany (the visit of the magi), while the Sunday following was recovered as a special celebration of the baptism of the Lord (the traditional Eastern Epiphany). But the Sundays in the period between January 6th and Ash Wednesday were termed "Sundays of the Year," a designation and numbering which were picked up again after Pentecost, and these two periods became popularly known as "Ordinary Time." The appointed lessons for these Sundays were simply readings in course without any special theme. There was however one minor exception in this reading in course: in Years A and B the Epiphany theme continued on the Second Sunday of the Year with readings featuring the Baptist's witness to the christological significance of Jesus' baptism as presented in the Fourth Gospel, while in Year C the reading on this Sunday was the Cana miracle, the changing of the water into wine, another traditional Epiphany theme.

This extension of the Epiphany theme provided a precedent for the Episcopal Church's adaptation of the three-year lectionary. We reverted to the designation of "Sundays after Epiphany," and retained in the calendar the not altogether appropriate term "Epiphany season" (it would be more correct to call it the "Season after Epiphany" analogous to the "Season after Pentecost"). The third change was the most important: regardless of the changing number of Sundays in this season, the last Sunday after Epiphany was made invariable, and the reading about the Transfiguration of the Lord was shifted from Lent 2 to this last Sunday. This was a stroke a genius on the part of the late Massey Shepherd (following earlier Lutheran precedent), and I well remember how the committee was electrified when he first suggested it. Adopting this proposal changed at a stroke the whole character of the season and imparted an epiphanic character to other readings falling between the first and last Sundays after Epiphany. This pattern of relevatory significance is succinctly expressed by the well-known hymn of Christopher Wordsworth, "Songs of thankfulness and praise," as revised by the late Bland Tucker (*The Hymnal 1982*, #135). We must however bear in mind that the readings between the first and last Sundays were originally designed as course readings of the Epistles and Gospels, with Old Testament readings to match the Gospels: the epiphanic motif was not originally intended, and it should not be forced upon readings where it is not appropriate. We will pay attention only to those readings which appear to be susceptible to an epiphanic interpretation.

Epiphany as a Hermeneutical Key

The word Epiphany and its cognate verb, to make manifest, occur very rarely in the New Testament. Most of these occurrences are in the Pastoral Epistles and nearly every time they refer to the second coming of Christ, the parousia. However, there are a number of closely associated words which are quite central to the New Testament, such as the verb "reveal" (*apokalýptō*), its cognate noun "revelation" (*apokálypsis*), and another word for "to make manifest" (*phaneróō*), as well as *phaínō*, "to shine." The important terms "light" (*phôs*) and "glory" (*dóxa*) are also used to describe what happened in the Christ event. Such terms indicate that we are clearly dealing here with concepts central to the biblical revelation.

All the words cited above are either metaphors or direct descriptions of the revelatory aspect of the Christ event, which is one of the basic types of New Testament Christology, though not the primary one. This revelatory Christology is celebrated in the Church Year from Advent through the Epiphany season. The primary Christology of the New Testament is redemptive or soteriological, and it is celebrated from Ash Wednesday through Pentecost. However, some of the course readings in the Epiphany season are soteriological rather than epiphanic. This is especially true of the series of readings from 1 Corinthians 15 which occur in Year C from Epiphany 5 through 8. Because these readings deal with the resurrection of believers and do not have an obviously epiphanic character, they will not be discussed in this article.

Three Modes of Epiphany

It is possible to discern three different types of epiphany in the readings for this season. Predominantly these readings speak of Christ as the epiphany to the world (christological epiphany). But there are also readings which speak of the church as an epiphany in its proclamation and common life (ecclesial epiphany). Thirdly, the Apostle Paul conceives his ministry as an epiphany (apostolic epiphany).

Christological Epiphany: The readings for January 6th, for Epiphany 1 and 2, and for the last Sunday of this season, all focus on the primary epiphany of the Christ event. The Old Testament readings are mainly from Isaianic promises of the light that should come into the world. The New Testament and Gospel readings on these occasions all attest to the Christ event as the fulfillment of this promise. Other christological epiphanies include the fulfillment quotation of Matthew 4:15–16 on Epiphany 3A ("the people who sat in darkness have seen a great light . . . light has dawned"). The dawn takes place with the beginning of the Galilean ministry with which the rest of the gospel readings will deal. In Year B Sundays 3–8 the readings are taken from the first two chapters of Mark.

Mark's Gospel has been described as a "book of secret epiphanies" (M. Dibelius). In his words and works Jesus reveals himself as the Messiah, but this revelation can be perceived only by faith and is not correctly understood until after the cross and resurrection. People who are healed are commanded to be silent; demons are silenced before they are driven out. The disciples misunderstand Jesus and are ordered to say nothing of what they have seen and heard until after the resurrection. Mark's secrecy motif is a reminder that the epiphany of God in Christ is not complete until Good Friday and Easter Day have occurred. The epiphanies during Jesus' earthly ministry are only prefigurations of the christological epiphany in its totality. The Christ event embraces the whole coming, ministry, death, and resurrection. Each particular event in the life of Christ points to its totality.

The Old Testament readings of the Epiphany season in Year B buttress those from Mark. Deuteronomy 18:15–20 (Epiphany 4B) promises that God will send a prophet like Moses. Jesus was interpreted originally as the prophet like Moses, the eschatological prophet, and Mark's miracle stories are formulated to express this Christology of Jesus as the eschatological prophet. This understanding is further expressed by the Old Testament readings for Epiphany 5B and 6B. On Epiphany 5B we read of the raising of the Shunammite woman's son, foreshadowing the raising of Simon's mother-in-law from her bed (Mark 1:29–31; NRSV misses the connection by translating *ēgeiren,* "raised" [v. 31], as merely "lifting" her up). On Epiphany 6B we read of the cure of Naaman of his leprosy (2 Kings 5:1–15b), foreshadowing the healing of the leper by Jesus (Mark 1:40–45). The reading from Hosea 2 on Epiphany 8B introduces the metaphor of marriage to express God's relationship with his people, thus matching the gospel reading in which Jesus' ministry represents the temporary appearance of the bridegroom, soon to be taken away (Mark 2:18–22). The Christ event is the fulfillment of Yahweh's promise to restore the nuptial relationship with Israel. It is the epiphany of the bridegroom.

Turning to Year C, we find that only two of the readings from Luke represent christological epiphanies, namely the two installments of Jesus' inaugural sermon in the synagogue at Nazareth on Epiphany 3C and 4C. The Lucan Jesus declares that the Isaianic prophecy of the anointed servant—one who will preach the good news, heal the sick, and raise the dead—is being fulfilled in his ministry. But then, like Elijah and Elisha, he is rejected by his own people and finds acceptance among the poor and the outcast, the marginalized in society, and finally, the Gentiles. The second part of the sermon thus strikes the note of universality, a motif already heard in the story of the magi on January 6th and a theme traditionally associated with Epiphany season. The Old Testament readings that accompany the inaugural sermon (Nehemiah 8:2–10 and Jeremiah 1:4–10) were chosen to match other points in the sermon—the public reading of scripture and the call to a prophetic mission, respectively. It would be forced exegesis to look for an explicit epiphany theme in these Old Testament readings.

Ecclesial Epiphany: Two striking features in the lectionary of this season are the readings from the Sermon on the Mount (Matthew) in Year A or on the Plain (Luke) in Year C, and the course readings in all three years from 1 Corinthians. There is a key verse in Matthew which highlights the epiphanic character of the church: "You are the light of the world" (Matthew 5:14). The great sermon can be understood as an exposition of the epiphanic character of the church, which is realized by the distinctiveness of its lifestyle. The church is a "contrast society" (G. Lohfinck). Note how Matthew adds four beatitudes to Luke's (and Q's) original four. These additional beatitudes have a more activistic character. The church consists of men and women who show mercy, who are pure in heart, who are peacemakers and reconcilers, who hunger after righteousness. (This is a good example of the way in which the preacher should pay particular attention to the theology of the evangelists as expressed in their redactional alteration of their sources. That is the whole point of having a Matthew, a Mark, and a Luke year!) The next distinctive feature in Matthew's version of the great sermon is the series of antitheses: "You have heard that it was said . . . but I say to you" (see Epiphany 6A, 7A). The contrast character of the church as epiphany is to be shown in the effort it makes to reconcile those within its fellowship who are at variance, by its higher standard of matrimonial fidelity(!), by a respect for truth, and so forth. Again, the final extract from the Sermon on the Mount, the teaching about anxiety (Epiphany 8A), urges the community to get its priorities right in its stewardship of material possessions.

Turning to Luke's Sermon on the Plain we find a somewhat different concern. Luke seeks to inculcate the values that are to permeate a community whose mission is to continue Jesus' preaching of the good news to the poor, the prisoners, and the brokenhearted. Note how Luke retains from Q the words "blessed are the poor," i.e., the economically poor, not those who are poor in spirit as in Matthew.

In all three years, as we have noted, most of the New Testament readings for this season are taken from 1 Corinthians. There is one curious exception. On two occasions in Year B (Epiphany 7 and 8) the readings are from 2 Corinthians. It is difficult to give an epiphanic interpretation to these two readings, and none will be attempted here.

Paul was always concerned that his churches should "shine like stars in the world" (Philippians 2:15) and nowhere more than in 1 Corinthians. The church in Corinth was afflicted by a false congregationalism and narrow parochialism. So Paul has to remind them that they are not the only Christian community in the world. They share a common life with many other local communities in other places: they are "called to be saints, together with those who in every place call on the name of our Lord Jesus Christ" (Epiphany 2A). Moreover, within their own fellowship they are splitting up into various cliques, each claiming loyalty to a different leader: "There are quarrels among you . . . each of you says 'I belong to Paul . . .' " (Epiphany 3A, cf. 6A). If the church is to be a true epiphany in its own locality, it must adapt itself to the particular society and culture in which it is placed. Like the apostle, the church has to adapt itself to its environment in order to win people for the gospel (see 1 Corinthians 9:16–23, Epiphany 5B). In other words, if it is to be a true epiphany, the church must be "inculturated"—to use a term popular among liturgiologists today. But such an endeavor has its dangers: one can take the process of inculturation too far, so that the church loses its distinctiveness and ceases to be a contrast society. This is what was happening in Corinth, where the believers were adopting too much from their Hellenistic environment, yielding to a triumphalist pride in their own wisdom. Paul seeks to bring home to them a more realistic understanding of their own position: "not many of you are wise by human standards . . . God chose what is weak in the world to shame the wise" (Epiphany 4A: see also the following two Sundays of Year A). The whole discussion culminates in a great epiphanic statement: "you are God's temple, and . . . God's Spirit dwells in you" (Epiphany 7A). To be a temple is to be the distinctive manifestation of God's presence in a non-Christian environment.

In Year B the reading of 1 Corinthians continues with a treatment of immorality among the believers (Epiphany 2B), a challenge to individuals who have failed to live out their Christian calling in their secular occupations (Epiphany 3B), and a call to the Christian community to respect the scruples of the weaker members within their own fellowship (Epiphany 4B). These topics may without straining the exegesis be interpreted in such a way as to relate them to the theme of ecclesial epiphany.

In Year C we move on to the later chapters of 1 Corinthians. The selections from chapters 12 and 14 (Epiphany 2C, 3C, and 4C) deal with the disunity in the church occasioned by the improper exercise of spiritual gifts *(charísmata)*, especially speaking in tongues. Those who had this latter gift thought it was the only one that really mattered, the criterion of genuine faith. Those who did not have it were despised as second-class Christians. Paul has to insist that all the gifts of the Spirit are equally important and that the criteria for their proper use are *agápē* and *oikodomé*, the building up of the body of Christ. Only so can the *charísmata* make the church an epiphany of Christ.

Apostolic Epiphany: A third form of epiphany is the ministry of Paul himself. At Corinth the apostle encountered certain expectations of what the apostolic ministry was. As becomes clearer in 2 Corinthians, the Christians in that church expected apostles to be spectacular preachers, spell-binding orators, with visions, miracles, and tongue-speaking to their credit (see especially 2 Corinthians 11–12). These expectations arose from the Hellenistic environment in which the Corinthians lived. It was common for wandering preachers to turn up in city after city, where they would display their powers and then pass the hat around for contributions from their audiences. In the face of this challenge, Paul, while recognizing that he could compete with the false apostles if he had a mind to, insists that the true epiphany of Christ is to be found in his apostolic labors and sufferings. Only these were epiphanies of the cross of Christ. The first rumblings of this controversy are already audible in 1 Corinthians in the readings appointed for Epiphany 8A, 5B, and 6B. Note how in 1 Corinthians 4:8–13 (Epiphany 8A) we have the first of several catalogues of sufferings (vv. 11-13), paving the way for the longer catalogues in 2 Corinthians. This emphasis on sufferings as epiphanies is analogous to the Marcan theme of the messianic secret. In 1 Corinthians 9:16–23 (Epiphany 5B) Paul explains his refusal to make money out of his preaching— for that would make him like the false preachers. His self-discipline was like that of an athlete in training, and this too was essential to a true understanding of apostolic ministry (1 Corinthians 9:24–27, Epiphany 6B).

Pre-Lent?

From time to time older Episcopalians who remember the BCP 1928 lament the loss of the old "gesima Sundays." In the current calendar Lent sometimes seems to creep up on us unawares. Occasionally, however, the readings for the later Sundays after Epiphany do present pre-Lenten themes. For instance, 1 Corinthians 9:24–27 (Epiphany 6B) and 1 Corinthians 12:27–13:13 (Last Epiphany C) are actually epistles of the old gesima Sundays which would give the preacher a chance to prepare for Lent. It should also be remembered, of course, that the Transfiguration readings appointed for every Last Epiphany provide a perfect opportunity to prepare the congregation for the Lenten pilgrimage to the cross.

Preaching in the Epiphany Season

It is not my intention to discuss the homiletic treatment of all the readings of this season (I have done this for the Roman Catholic version of the three-year lectionary elsewhere). However, a few examples may be given of the way in which the three types of epiphany—christological, ecclesial, and apostolic—may be applied to the contemporary situation in the church. Of course, each local congregation has its own specific circumstances, and only the preacher who knows what they are can speak to them effectively. Here we must confine ourselves to situations which face the church in general.

Christological Epiphany: Throughout the year all Christian preaching is basically a proclamation of the Christ event. In the Easter portion of the church year, i.e. from Ash Wednesday to Pentecost, the Christ event is proclaimed in its redemptive aspect, focusing on the paschal mystery, the death and resurrection of Christ. From Advent through the Epiphany season the same event is proclaimed in terms of revelation, of "God in man made manifest." This difference of presentation of the Christ event, as we have already noted, goes back to the New Testament itself. The two modes of presentation do not represent contradictory approaches but different ways of envisioning the same christological event.

Perhaps the central focus of the christological epiphany is its universal character, traditionally seen in the magi story on January 6th, but also emphasized in the second part of the inaugural sermon at Nazareth on Epiphany 4C. We live in an age in which there is considerable embarrassment about the universality, uniqueness, and finality of the Christ event. These sorts of questions are raised by such considerations as post-holocaust consciousness of the way Jews have been treated in the past, the influx into the Western world of numerous people of Moslem faith, and the attraction of Eastern religions—especially Buddhism—felt by many of the younger generation. In response to these challenges some theologians are arguing for a position of near relativism. Christianity, it is proposed, is just one among other religions, all of which are equally valid ways of communing with the Transcendent.

Most of the difficulty is due to thinking of "Christianity" as a religion. The very word Christianity is not a biblical concept. Christianity is largely what we have made in response to the Christ event. The Bible proclaims that event as something that really happened. Nothing in the world can make it unhappen. As an event it shares in the "scandal of particularity." The whole point of the Christ event is that the universal is encapsulated in a particular human life; the Transcendent has become uniquely immanent. To deny or qualify this is to reject the fundamental message of the Bible, which is rooted in Jesus' preaching of the eschatological kingdom of God. True, the Transcendent was already manifested "in many and various ways" (Hebrews 1:1). The Transcendent was already "the light of all people" (John 1:4). "But in these last days" [i.e., eschatologically] God "has spoken to us by a Son" (Hebrews 1:1). In this Son, the Word (i.e. the Transcendent which was already apprehended partially by all human beings) has become flesh, enclosed in a human life.

This is the basic gospel of the Epiphany season. It is the driving force behind the "decade of Evangelism." We are not seeking to convert the world to Christianity as a Western religion, but to bear witness to the universal, unique, and final reality of the Christ event. That is the purpose behind the preaching of the christological epiphany in this season.

Ecclesial Epiphany: The conflicting claim of inculturation on the one hand, and the church's vocation to be a contrast society on the other, present us with an acute dilemma. What does the challenge mean for such issues as sexuality, ecology, and peace, or for the relation between church and politics or economics? In one way or another all these issues are posed by the seasonal readings from the Sermon on the Mount in Year A, and some of them in the Sermon on the Plain in Year C. And what does it mean to be a contrast society in an urban, suburban, or rural environment?

The readings from 1 Corinthians 1–4 and 12–14 provide a useful opportunity to deal with unity and disunity in the local congregation. This emphasis may be particularly pertinent in congregations which have experienced charismatic renewal. Are there some members who claim that certain gifts, like speaking in tongues, are essential to Christian experience, and that those who do not speak in tongues are second-class Christians?

The Epiphany season always includes the Octave of Prayer for Christian Unity (January 18–25). Paul's concern for the unity of the local church with the universal church on the one hand, and for the inner unity between groups and cliques of the local community on the other, raises issues which are acute for Episcopalians and for the whole Anglican communion today. How far is the Episcopal church in the USA entitled to "go it alone"?

Apostolic Epiphany: In the controversy which still goes on about the ordination of women, traditionalists often use the "icon argument." They contend that since the priest represents Christ at the altar and since Christ was a male, the priest therefore must be male. Paul would agree that an apostolic minister is the icon of Christ. But this icon is expressed not in the male sex of the apostle but in his labors and sufferings. These alone make him an epiphany of the cross of Christ. Who could argue that only men are capable of apostolic labors and sufferings and that therefore only men are capable of being icons or epiphanies of Christ?

In short, whether the preacher chooses to emphasize christological epiphany, ecclesial epiphany, or apostolic epiphany, the readings for this season offer ample homiletical material. Rather than being a tedious stretch of "ordinary time," the Sundays after Epiphany provide an extraordinary opportunity to proclaim the good news of God made known in Jesus Christ.

Lent

Daniel B. Stevick

SERMONS DURING LENT are often planned rather carefully by preachers and listened to with more than ordinary attention by congregations. Preachers will find a considerable measure of consistency of theme and tone in the Prayer Book provision for the five Sundays of the season. However, some of the Lenten emphases still surprise many persons whose sense of the season was formed by former liturgies and older pieties. Unless the Prayer Book intentions for Lent are understood, a homiletic opportunity will be missed.

Origin of Lent

The exhortation in the Ash Wednesday liturgy (BCP, pp. 264–265) bids us to observe the season "by self-examination and repentance; by prayer, fasting, and self-denial; and by reading and meditating on God's holy Word." Such penitential themes have for centuries, with varying degrees of intensity, formed the principal thrust of Lent. They remain important. The "Litany of Penitence" (BCP, pp. 267–69) sets a tone of contrite self-examination. The weekdays of the season are to be observed "by special acts of discipline and self-denial" (BCP, p. 17). However, the informative, inviting, and yet serious Ash Wednesday exhortation speaks of "the early Christians," suggesting that the liturgies of the 20th century have reproportioned Lenten emphases along lines suggested by history.

In the early centuries, the pre-Easter weeks were not dominated by penitence. The only yearly observance in the earliest Christian community was Easter. It was based, in time and in theme, on the Jewish Passover. As Passover spoke of the exodus from Egypt, Easter spoke of emancipation from the bondage of sin and death through Jesus' death and resurrection. It proclaimed the breaking in of the new age of the Spirit, whose sign-community is the church. The day itself led to a sustained celebratory season of fifty days, lasting until Pentecost, marking the risen Christ living among his people.

This yearly celebration of the heart of the redemptive saga was also ordinarily the one time in the year for baptism. The death and resurrection of Jesus was replicated in the death and rebirth of new Christians. Initially there was no Holy Week, observing the events between Jesus' final entry into Jerusalem and his burial; the early church did not approach liturgical time with our somewhat biographical style of thought. The period before Easter centered on the candidates for baptism—the "catechumens," persons who were receiving instruction, taking part in works of charity, and attending the Sunday liturgy regularly, although only for the Service of the Word.

As Easter drew near, the catechumens who were judged to be ready for baptism were given special instruction and assigned special austerities. Confession of sin was a part of coming to baptism, but the event as a whole was suffused with joy. The Christians who were already baptized (many of whom would themselves have previously gone through a similar educational and ritual process) shared to some extent in these exercises of readiness. Baptism was an event for the church, not just for the individual. The weeks prior to Easter were given to the vitalizing and demanding task of getting the catechumens ready for baptism.

In the early centuries, penance did come to occupy some of the congregation's attention prior to Easter. Persons who had brought scandal on the community of faith were forbidden to receive communion. Offenders who sought to return were made "penitents," who followed a regimen of prayer and fasting, sackcloth and ashes (supported by the intercessions of the church), and attendance only at the early part of the Sunday eucharist. When they were judged to be ready, they were restored to full standing in the church at Easter. Their "second repentance" thus followed the same time period and was brought to its conclusion in the same ritual event as was the admission of the catechumens at Easter baptism.

A Change in Character

By the 5th or 6th centuries, most people in the population centers of the Mediterranean basin had become Christian. The catechumenate largely disappeared, and baptism came to center on the children of Christian parents. The Easter restoration of persons under discipline, however, continued. Following the collapse of the Roman Empire, people internalized the disorder of the world around them, and a mood of widespread gloom came over the society. The emphasis of the period preceding Easter shifted from preparing eager catechumens for baptism to lamenting the sins of Christians. The length of the season was set at forty days, and a connection was made with Jesus' time in the wilderness (Mark 1:13 and parallels). With general restraints on common pleasures and much emphasis on human frailty, Lent became not so much a season of looking forward to Easter as it was an extension backward of Good Friday.

This severely penitential Lent persisted through the Middle Ages (lengthened by some pre-Lenten weeks) and was inherited by the liturgical communions of the modern world. The 1928 Prayer Book designated the week prior to Holy Week as beginning "Passiontide." The 1940 Hymnal provided 34 hymns for Lent and Passiontide (plus 49 in a list of other suitable hymns outside the Lent section). By contrast, it had 17 hymns for Easter, which was evidently taken to be a single day (or at most an octave) rather than a celebrational season which included seven Sundays. The loss of the Vigil and of baptisms at Easter throughout the West, the neglect of "the great Fifty Days," and the Lenten preoccupation with contrition and cross-centered piety are liturgical aspects of what one writer called "the lost radiance of the Christian religion."

Sin and Grace

We should not only think about Lent historically; we must also think theologically about the reality to which the season bears witness. As the early church, in its liturgy and discipline, was serious about sin, so we should be. Sin is a terrible, destructive reality. When one considers the individual and collective sins of our time, "the burden of them is intolerable." We find ways of excusing ourselves, justifying ourselves, of deceiving ourselves about ourselves and about the world we have made. The scriptures, the preaching, and the liturgy of Lent all seek to help us toward a sense of moral reality, even though we resist.

While being serious about sin, we need also to keep the proportion set by the Christian gospel. Although sin is real, it does not have the last word. We appraise sinfulness from the point of view of the good news. In a sense, sin is part of the gospel, just as Lent is part of the year of grace.

It is good news that we speak of "the fall." The myth implies that things as they are are not things as they were meant to be. We live in an order gone wrong—an alienated, distorted order, whose distortion we internalize. But God did not intend it so.

It is similarly good news that we identify our problem as "sin." "Sin" is a religious term, speaking of a relation to God. It is a term usable and significant only to faith. If we anatomize human destructiveness and folly from secular viewpoints, our "deadly sins updated" yield principally the tragic view of life and lead to despair. A Christian sense of sin is not a conclusion from the contradictions of the human condition. Sin arises because we live in relation to God—a relation given with life itself. An awareness of God (unless it is simply a comfortable god of our own making) includes an awareness of a violation of that relation. Reality is so ordered that sin which is against God is also against others and ourselves.

In the face of human sin, God judges, and divine judgment too is good news. A God who judges is not indifferent. God cares— cares righteously and passionately. Judgment says that our actions matter; our motives for acting matter; we matter. Judgment is an index of worth!

A radical wrong requires a radical remaking. The New Testament uses drastic metaphors—such as dying and being born again. It speaks of a remaking for which our own resources are inadequate, and it offers grace. "Where sin increased, grace abounded all the more" (Romans 5:20b). Into our distorted order, a good news comes—a news too good to be true if it were not true. This news witnesses to an alternative reality. It offers the true order of life and love.

That news frees us to identify sin. The sense of sin, in Christian terms, depends on that which transcends sin. Knowledge of the distance that separates us from God is a gift of faith and revelation. The good news is not that we sin. Sin is always a negation. The good news is that we can name sin and deal with it in a community of forgiven and forgiving people. We are given the courage to face sin, always in touch with the grace which exceeds it. One notes a paradox: we only become aware of sin in the light of the very thing which assures us that sin is no longer our ultimate problem.

Thus talk of sin is characteristically the in-talk of the community of faith. It is not a useful accusation to make against the unbelieving world. Apart from faith, one lacks the capacity to recognize sin.

The point for Lent is that God is the primary reality. Although our sin is a terrible negation, it is caught up in God's creative purposes, impartial omnipotent love, sacrificial divine involvement, and ultimate triumph. God is able to take up and utilize the negation in carrying out, at personal cost, the work of redemption. As Christians observing Lent, we do not fall out of the good news for forty days each spring, only to become reattached at the Easter Vigil. A pedal note of redemption sounds all through the year—in the seasons of penitence as much as in the seasons of festival.

Daniel B. Stevick

The Lenten Lections

The lectionary provision for Lent is rich and varied. The liturgy for Ash Wednesday is searching: a call to repentance from the prophet Joel, Paul's anguished plea that his readers be reconciled with God, Jesus' directions about secret fasting, Psalm 51 (the profoundest of the penitential psalms), and a Litany of Penitence.

As the season develops, however, the lectionary does not draw attention to the sins of Christians. In congregations where there are adult catechumens, the pastoral actions of "The Catechumenate" (in *The Book of Occasional Services*) will mark and interpret the season; but in all congregations the baptized are preparing for the Easter recalling of redemption and the new baptismal life. The preparatory weeks have once again been made a time of instruction and upbuilding as the church prepares through attention to great scriptural themes.

In all three lectionary years, the Gospel for Lent 1 is the story of Jesus' temptation. The accounts are obviously symbolic. Jesus entertains and dismisses three available and attractive types of Messiahship. He will not base his leadership on supplying material needs, on dazzling wonders which put God on the spot, or on political empire. He will refashion Messiahship in ways which eventually will lead him to a cross.

In Year A, Jesus' temptation is linked with the story of the fall in the Garden of Eden (Genesis 2:4b–3:7). His successful holding off of the tempter begins the undoing of the mischief of which the primal yielding by Adam and Eve is a symbol. In this same year, Paul's parallel and contrast between Christ and Adam in Romans 5 is read. Both names stand for great human solidarities, one in condemnation and death, the other in righteousness and life. But they are not equal and opposite. Adam is a "type" or shadow, pointing to the prior and greater reality of Christ. Redemption in Christ is the fully adequate reversal of the calamitous loss represented by Adam.

In Year B, Jesus' temptation is told in Mark's summary account, and the reading includes Jesus' baptism as well. The baptism is linked to the development in the liturgical Epistle (1 Peter 3:18–22, a somewhat obscure passage) of the story of Noah and rescue from the flood as illustrative of Christian baptism. The first reading tells of God's covenant with Noah—a covenant of faithfulness and new beginning (made with nature as well as with humanity) arising out of judgment and destruction.

In Year C, Luke's story of the temptation is preceded by the rich material about salvation of Romans 10:5–13. A link between the two may well be Paul's "the word is near" theme which suggests Jesus' parrying the tempter with the Word of God.

No other Sunday in the season has a theme that runs through all three years. Rather, in the scripture material one can identify clusters which come from similar sources or express related themes.

One such cluster is the seven readings from John that fall on three Sundays of the A and B years. There is no "John year" in the lectionary, but johannine material is worked into all three years to give its distinctive point of view at appropriate moments. Thinking of the catechumens, with joy of conversion upon them, and of the catechumenal church of the 20th century, we have from John seven pericopes: being born again (Lent 2, Year A), Jesus meeting the woman at the well and speaking of himself as the living water (Lent 3, Year A), Jesus' body as the true Temple (Lent 3, Year B), the healing of the man born blind and Jesus as light of the world (Lent 4, Year A), the sign of the bread (Lent 4, Year B), the raising of Lazarus and Jesus as the resurrection and the life (Lent 5, Year A), and Jesus' final summing up of his public ministry, including his statement about the grain which does not multiply until it "dies" (Lent 5, Year B). The story of Lazarus is matched with a first reading about the dry bones (representing Israel) which come to life as Ezekiel prophesies, and flesh and breath return to them. Jesus' signs of transformation and his Christological affirmations conduct us into the heart of the johannine presentation of Christ. They interpret baptism as birth from above, as passage from blindness to sight and from death to life; and they exhibit the way into which one is brought by baptism as drinking the water of life and eating the bread from heaven.

Seven of the epistle readings for the season come from Romans, and five of them in Years A and B are from Romans chapters 5–8, a passage which the late John Knox called "the most serious and successful effort any New Testament writer makes to describe from within the life in Christ." Abraham believes God's promise (4:1–17; Lent 2, Year A). Christ is the answer to Adam (5:12–21; Lent 1, Year A). We are justified by faith (5:1–11; Lent 3, Year A, as well as 10:5–13, Ash Wednesday, Year C). Those who were slaves of sin and paid by death have become servants of God and have the gift of life (6:16–23; Lent 5, Year A). Paul asks, "Who will deliver me?" And he answers his own question, "Thanks be to God through Jesus Christ our Lord!" (7:13–25; Lent 3, Year B). We are more than conquerors (8:31–39; Lent 2, Year B). This is catechetical material of first-rank importance. Persons preparing for baptism need to know it; all Christians need to hear it again.

Converts are stepping into a new life; they should become familiar with paradigmatic persons who have pioneered the venture of faith. From the scriptures of Israel the lectionary provides two "call stories"—the call of Abraham (Lent 2, Year A [Abraham's call is linked with Paul's interpretation of it in Romans 4:1–17; Abraham was justified by trusting God's promise]), and the call of Moses (Lent 3, Year C). As further model, Abraham's radical obedience under radical testing is encountered (Lent 2, Year B) in the story of his willingness to sacrifice Isaac. The baptized will be anointed—brought into a community of royalty—and the lectionary tells of the anointing of David (Lent 4, Year A).

The readings, however, do not just give stories of individuals. The converts are entering a collective life which has a history—a covenant people which lives by promise. The appointed lessons are full of the theme of covenant: God's covenant with Noah (Lent 1, Year B) and with Abraham (Lent 2, Year C), and the promise in Jeremiah of a new and inward covenant (Lent 5, Year B). Crucial events in the history of Israel are read to speak of life in the new Israel, suggesting a typological mode of interpretation. The church is a people of the exodus, and the capsule recounting of Israel's captivity and release, "a wandering Aramaean . . . ," is read on Lent 1, Year C. The church is a community under divine discipline, and the first reading of Lent 3, Year B, tells of the giving of the ten commandments—long a staple of baptismal instruction. The Christians are a people in exile, as the first reading of Lent 4, Year B, which tells of Judah taken into captivity, would remind them. The story of Joshua leading the people into Canaan falls on Lent 4, Year C. Christians have in faith come into the land of promise; parts of the early church used a chalice of milk and honey at the baptismal eucharist. The promises are yours.

Luke's Gospel is the longest, and all of the Lenten Gospel readings in Year C are from Luke. Two severe lessons come from chapter 13: the narrow door that leads to salvation and Jesus' "O Jerusalem" lament on Lent 2, and his urgent "repent or perish" on Lent 3. On Lent 4 the church reads from Luke 15:11–32 the parable that might appropriately be called "the prodigal father." In this longest of Jesus' parables, God is depicted as setting his children free, and when they bring ruin on themselves and recognize it, taking them back without conditions or recrimination. The two sons mark this as one of Jesus' parables of contrast; the son who never left home must also come to terms with the father's compassion. The tone of severity returns on Lent 5 with the story of the rebellious tenants (Luke 20:9–19). When one examines this story of far-off rural life, one realizes that it is a Galilean gothic tale of horror.

A few readings which do not seem to belong in these clusters are nonetheless important for the catechumens and the congregation. The Gospel for Lent 2 in Year B is Jesus' startling announcement in Mark 8 that he will suffer and die and rise again. On Lent 3, Year C, in the second lesson, Paul (1 Corinthians 10:1–13) recalls Israel in the wilderness and says "Do not presume." Two lections for Lent 4 come from Ephesians. One (2:4–10, Year A) depicts believers as alive in Christ. Appropriately for persons coming to baptism, the other (5:1–14, Year B) speaks of passing from one way of life to another, from darkness to light. The early Christians frequently spoke of baptism as "illumination" or "enlightenment." On Lent 5, Year B, Hebrews 5:1–10 speaks of Christ as heavenly high priest—a compassionate priest because he himself knew human struggle and suffering. His obedience was learned. Philippians is drawn on twice. On Lent 5, Year C, Paul, alluding to his own conversion, speaks of Christ as worth the loss of all things (3:8–14), and on Lent 2, Year C, the theme is the Christian's true commonwealth in heaven (3:17–4:1).

In both its continuing themes and its occasional readings of singular power, this liturgical provision of lections sets a tone by which God's faithful people can "prepare with joy for the Paschal feast" (second Preface for Lent, BCP, p. 379).

Holy Week

Charles P. Price

THE OBSERVANCES OF HOLY WEEK according to the Book of Common Prayer begin on Palm Sunday and end on Holy Saturday (the Easter Vigil is part of the Easter celebration). Proper liturgies are provided for Palm Sunday, Maundy Thursday, Good Friday, and Holy Saturday. Proper collects and lections are appointed in the Lectionary for Monday, Tuesday, and Wednesday. Normally there will be a service on every day of this week, and the Prayer Book envisions a sermon or homily at each service except Holy Saturday, when a homily is optional.

To fulfill that expectation is the most daunting challenge which a preacher faces in the course of the Church Year. It demands prayer, hard work, and immersion in the agony of the world; and in the end the right words will be found only through the grace of God.

Some Fundamental Considerations

During Holy Week the preacher needs to be especially sensitive to the nature of Christian liturgy and liturgical time. Liturgy in any season of the Church calendar is an *anamnesis* or memorial of the death and resurrection of Christ, making effective in the present an event in the past. It is God, to be sure, whose presence in the church's worship enables the presencing of these past events. No esoteric human capacity to remember is involved.

This point is especially pertinent to the Holy Week liturgy, for these services are not simply historical commemorations of Jesus' suffering and death, as events of an ever-more-remote antiquity. They are much more witnesses to the power of his victory in the present. In the primitive church, the Christian Passover (Pascha) was the unitive celebration of the suffering, death, and victory of the Son of God. These events were celebrated together, and their effects were experienced together. In the course of time, celebrations were spread over the whole week, with different motifs becoming prominent on successive days. Each celebration became an *anamnesis* of "Christ's Victory and Ours" (to use the title of Frederick Grant's meditations on the passion from a generation ago), but each acquired a different nuance because of the historical events commemorated on that day. Subsequently Christian celebrations covered the entire year, always as anamneses of the death and resurrection of the Lord.

Although some of them were unfamiliar to twentieth-century Episcopalians, most of the provisions in the 1979 Prayer Book are in fact very old. In a diary of her pilgrimage to the Holy Land in the second half of the fourth century, that redoubtable Spanish nun, Egeria, describes taking part in the observances of the Christian community in Jerusalem during one Holy Week—the Palm Sunday procession from the Mount of Olives, the Thursday afternoon Eucharist, the veneration of the cross on Friday. She did not herself record the passages of Scripture which were read; but we know from other sources that a number of the lections appointed for these days in our Proper Liturgies appeared in the earliest lectionaries. Because of the character of liturgical time, the choice of lessons at these earliest celebrations was not constrained by the historical sequence of events. On Palm Sunday not only is the story of the triumphal entrance read, but also the whole narrative of the passion; and to make it impossible to mistake the character of the occasion as an anamnesis of the cross and resurrection, the epistle has traditionally been the hymn of the humiliation and exaltation of Christ from Philippians 2. On Maundy Thursday, not only is St. Paul's account of the supper read, with its eschatological reference (". . . until he comes"), but also the Johannine account, with no words over bread or wine, and no command to repeat it.

A preacher sympathetic to this character of liturgical time can turn these multi-layered references to advantage. One way to proceed can be learned from observing how medieval and Renaissance painters depicted biblical scenes. They made no pretence of historical accuracy. They often painted the crucifixion, for example, with all the participants in medieval or Renaissance dress, with buildings as contemporary as the clothes, and scenery which would be familiar to local viewers. Preachers might take a hint from this practice and think about narrating the stories of the passion in contemporary dress, as if they were happening before their hearers' eyes. It would increase a congregation's sense of participation, so that worshipers could then answer the words of the Good Friday hymn, "Yes, we were there when they crucified our Lord."

It seems useful to suggest that during Holy Week if not at all times preachers should be prepared to preach in at least two different ways. The first kind of utterance, conventionally called a sermon, may be conceived as fuller, more formal, usually longer. The second kind, conventionally called a homily, is terse, direct, with a minimum of elaboration or embroidery, the homiletical counterpart of an "arrow prayer." Preachers should probably deliver themselves of sermons on Palm Sunday, Maundy Thursday (*pace* the rubric), and Good Friday; and of homilies on Monday, Tuesday, Wednesday and Saturday.

There will, of course, be exceptions to this rule. If there are noonday preaching services during Holy Week, for example, there will be sermons rather than homilies on Monday, Tuesday, and Wednesday. Early morning celebrations with few in attendance invite homilies rather than sermons. This pattern does not give the preacher license to do less work, however; homilies take as much preparation as sermons.

Charles P. Price 81

The Sunday of the Passion: Palm Sunday

In the 1979 Prayer Book the first and therefore primary name of the Sunday before Easter is The Sunday of the Passion. Palm Sunday is its secondary title. These two names point to two liturgical emphases. One is represented by the Liturgy of the Palms, with its reading of the account of Jesus entering Jerusalem, hailed as Messiah by the crowds gathered along the way. The other emphasis is represented in the Eucharist, where the Service of the Word (and in fact the whole Palm Sunday service) is dominated by the passion story: Matthew in Year A, Mark in Year B, Luke in Year C. (The Passion according to John is reserved for Good Friday, in accordance with the ancient tradition.) The Sunday of the Passion commemorates both the triumphal entry and the crucifixion.

The challenge to the preacher is to establish the inner connection between these two events. How could the excited, tumultuous acclamation accorded to Jesus when he entered the city lead without a struggle to his betrayal, desertion, and crucifixion a few days later?

The shouts of the crowd on Palm Sunday must have been a messianic greeting. "Hosanna to the Son of David! Blessed is he who comes in the name of the Lord!" (Matthew 21:9; Mark and Luke report slight variants.) The crowds seem to have expected a fighter who would lead armed resistance to Roman occupation. Peter himself apparently had the same expectation when he called Jesus the Christ at Caesarea Philippi (Mark 8:29). Peter had a more popular and aggressive understanding of messiahship than Jesus did. Jesus refused to accept the popular idea, out of obedience to the vocation from his heavenly Father which he was coming more and more to understand. Matters came to a head on Palm Sunday. Jesus did not fulfill what the crowd expected of him; and when the Pharisees charged him with claiming to be the Messiah, a crime worthy of death, the crowd turned against him in disappointed rage.

A preacher might explore the short-lived character of all earthly triumph. As the palms of Palm Sunday are burned to make ashes for Ash Wednesday imposition, so our greatest human triumphs and successes will fail to sustain us unless we are obedient to God in achieving them. They rather bring us to a cross. It is a liturgical and homiletical error to regard Jesus' triumphal entry as an occasion of unreserved joy for Christian worshipers. Worshipers know the end of the story. The reading of a synoptic passion narrative guarantees it. Palm Sunday is a time of irony, sadness, and wonder at the mysterious ways of God in human history. The proper color of its hangings is red—not the brilliant red of Pentecost but the blood-red of the cross.

The preacher has other options. A striking sermon would look at the cross through the eyes of those who took part in those events: Mary, Peter, the maid at the high priest's palace, Pilate, Simon of Cyrene, Jewish priests, Roman soldiers, faithless disciples. It is a kaleidoscopic *dramatis personae*. The preacher must be careful, of course, not to inflame anti-Jewish sentiments. The story is told to convict its present hearers, not someone else. Priests, soldiers, disciples, all should be clad in modern dress. When we can put ourselves in the place of the priests, we will see the inadequacy and failure of *our* religion, which brought the Son of God to this end. When we put ourselves in the place of soldiers, we see the failure of *our* political power, which inflicts such suffering on weak and innocent people. When we remember that the disciples "forsook him and fled," we acknowledge the failure of *our* discipleship. "Then what becomes of our boasting? It is excluded" (Romans 3:27).

Another sermon could be based on Jesus' words from the cross. In Matthew and Mark, there is only one desolate word, "My God, my God, why hast thou forsaken me?" That text would compel the preacher to treat the full humanity of Jesus, the bitterness of his dying, the reality of dust and blood. Every human sufferer can make common cause with him. In this approach, however, one must also consider the weight of Psalm 22 in Matthew's and Mark's telling of the passion story. Jesus' word from the cross is a citation of its first verse, and several features of these two accounts of the crucifixion—the agony of his death, the division of his garments, the casting of lots—seem to be colored if not dictated by it. In the Psalm the sufferer nevertheless trusts in God, and the end of the Psalm is an overwhelming vision of God's universal and everlasting rule. "The kingdom is the Lord's . . ."

The words of Jesus in Luke are different: to the soldiers, "Father, forgive them, for they know not what they do"; to the penitent criminal, "This day you shall be with me in Paradise"; and to God, "Father, into your hands I commit my spirit." A sermon on the Lukan version of Jesus' dying words would be quite different from the Matthean-Markan one. It would fasten hearts and minds on the nearness of God's forgiveness, the power of repentance, and the victorious resignation of trusting in God's rule over the world, and over us.

No sermon on the crucifixion may treat it objectively. In the cross our lives, our world, our history, come under judgment, no matter how great our triumph on some preceding Palm Sunday.

Monday, Tuesday and Wednesday in Holy Week

The lections appointed for Monday through Wednesday in Holy Week are the same in each year of the three-year cycle.

Gospels: The preferred gospel reading on each of these days is a pericope from the Fourth Gospel, setting the tone for the Johannine readings on Maundy Thursday and Good Friday. Monday's reading (John 12:1–11) is the account of Mary's anointing of Jesus' feet with "costly ointment." The context makes it clear that John understands this Mary to be the sister of Martha and Lazarus. Tuesday's lection (John 12:37–38, 42–50) represents a final call for decision. "He who believes in me, believes not in me but in him who sent me" (v.44). On Wednesday we hear the account of Jesus' quiet recognition at the Last Supper of Judas' betrayal (John 13:21–35).

Again it should be noted that no effort is made in these selections to represent the historical sequence of events. In the Johannine order, Mary's anointing of Jesus occurs before Palm Sunday, and the recognition of Judas' betrayal takes place after the Maundy Thursday foot-washing. Nevertheless this sequence suggests several homiletical opportunities. On Monday, the contrast between Mary's lavish devotion and Judas' hard stinginess masked by charity ("Why was this ointment not sold for three hundred denarii and given to the poor?" John 12:5), could open a rich vein of comments on faith and generosity. Mary's act as a poignant recognition of Jesus' messiahship following the raising of Lazarus should not be overlooked, nor its significance as a foreshadowing of the Messiah's death and burial.

Contemporary applications of Tuesday's lection—a study of those who have come to believe in Jesus and those who have not—lie ready at hand. Who among us can recognize that God's decision for the world has already occurred in the life and teaching of the Lord? Who can see that our judgment on him is God's judgment on us? Who will not admit that we too have "loved the praise of men more than the praise of God"? Who will be constant in the coming test? Have we not all fallen short? Do we not all need the forgiveness of God? (cf. Romans 3:22.)

The fascinating figure of Judas, who appears in both Monday's and Wednesday's readings, invites imaginative narrative preaching. How is the preacher to present the motives for Judas' behavior? Greed? Disappointed messianic expectations? The terrible hardening of some human hearts in the face of purity and truth? The mysterious Providence of God? If the preacher can make a plausible case for Judas, hearers will be helped to find those recesses of their own hearts where similar darkness lurks. It is a task worthy of Holy Week.

An alternative Gospel is appointed on each of these three days. The alternatives on Monday and Wednesday are the synoptic variants of Johannine provisions (Mark 14:1–9, Matthew 26:1–5, 14–25). Tuesday's gospel reading (Mark 11:15–19) is the cleansing of the temple, an incident reported in the Fourth Gospel in quite a different connection, at the beginning of Jesus' ministry. Like the Palm Sunday entry, it is a messianic sign (cf Mal 3:1), and if read, might be treated as an extension of the Palm Sunday gospel.

Old Testament Lessons: On these three days of Holy Week three of the four Songs of the Servant from Second Isaiah are read in succession. The fourth Song is the preferred Old Testament reading for Good Friday. It would be a welcome and profitable change from sermons on the gospel lessons to preach, say one year in three, on this sequence of readings from Isaiah.

A starting point for such a series of sermons might be the observation that the expressions of the Servant's suffering grow deeper and more searching with each song. On Monday, his patience, on Tuesday his despair, on Wednesday his pain. On Monday, the suffering of the Servant is seen in connection with a call to work for justice in the world:

I have put my Spirit upon him,
he will bring forth justice to the nations . . .
(Isaiah 42:1, cf. 42:4)

The church is called to work and suffer for justice under the cross. On Tuesday, God gives the suffering One "as a light to the nations" (Isaiah 49:6). Here is an opportunity to address in the light of the cross the church's mission amid its travail and despair. On Wednesday in the reading from Isaiah 50, the Servant "gave his back to the smiters and his cheeks to those who pulled out the beard." God opens the ear of the Servant and steels him to face his tormentors with confidence and hope. Here the theme might be the cross and Christian boldness.

Psalms: The Psalms of the Passion constitute a rewarding source of material which preachers often overlook. The verses from Psalm 36 on Monday would invite a sermon on the towering love of God in the face of the looming mystery of the cross. "Your love, O Lord, reaches to the heavens . . . For with you is the well of life, and in your light we see light . . ." (Psalm 36:5,9).

Tuesday's psalm, Psalm 71:1–12, is a expression of hope and confidence, with a verse which the Holy Week context sharpens and deepens: "I have become a portent to many; but you are my refuge and strength" (Psalm 71:7). In the face of the cross, no situation is so evil, no rejection so final, that God cannot turn it to good. The end is praise. "Let my mouth be full of your praise and your glory all the day long" (Psalm 71:8). Wednesday brings the cross still closer: "They gave me gall to eat, and when I was thirsty, they gave me vinegar to drink" (Psalm 69:23). This psalm is a heartbreaking prayer for the mercy of God in the face of torture; and the appointed verses, like the cross itself on Good Friday, stop short of an answer. This psalm would suggest a sermon on suffering which has no obvious relief. "The waters have risen up to my neck." "From where is my help to come?"

Maundy Thursday

From the time of the earliest Roman lectionaries, the epistle appointed for the evening celebration of Eucharist on Thursday of Holy Week has been Paul's account of the institution of the Supper (I Corinthians 11:20–32) and the gospel reading has been John's account of Jesus' washing of the disciples' feet. The name *Maundy* is derived from the Latin word, *mandatum*, commandment; it is a reference to the text, "A new commandment I give you, that you love one another even as I have loved you" (John 13:34), used as an antiphon in the ancient liturgy (cf. Marion Hatchett, *Commentary on the American Prayer Book* [New York: Seabury Press, 1980], p. 229).

The preacher on Maundy Thursday has to deal with two irreconcilable traditions. Words over bread and wine are the centerpiece of the synoptic tradition; Paul and Luke add the command, "Do this in remembrance of me," instituting the Eucharist. John has no account of words spoken over bread and wine at the Supper, and the only commandment to institute a liturgical action has to do with footwashing: "If I then, your Lord and Teacher, have washed your feet, you also ought to wash one another's feet" (John 13:14). The long Johannine discourses (John 13–17) have no counterpart in the synoptic gospels. Once more, we notice that no effort has been made in these ancient liturgical provisions to secure historical consistency. Instead, the preacher finds a full plate of historical allusions and a wealth of operative images.

Whether the preacher chooses to emphasize the institution of the Eucharist or the footwashing, it is an occasion to underline the character of the sacrament as providing worshipers with a means for taking part again and again in "those mighty acts, whereby you

Charles P. Price   87

have given us life and immortality" (Collect for the Liturgy of the Palms, BCP, p. 270). Participation through sacramental action is a unifying motif of this complex Maundy Thursday celebration.

The Last Supper was a Passover meal according to the synoptic tradition; and even if one prefers the Johannine chronology, which assigns the Supper to the evening before the Passover (cf. John 18:28), Passover themes would have been in the air. The whole character of the sacramental life of Israel, which remembered its past history in the presence of God, and so appropriated the present power of those events, becomes available to inform the preacher's development. The Old Testament lesson (Exodus 1:14a), for example, refers to the Passover as "a memorial day," an anamnesis. Israel claimed that "not with our fathers did the Lord make this covenant, but with *us*" (Deuteronomy 5:3), that *"we* were Pharaoh's slaves in Egypt and the Lord brought *us* out of Egypt with a mighty hand" (Deuteronomy 6:21). If a congregation can be helped to see and participate in this sacramental sense of remembered history and feel the present power of these past events in its anamnesis, then indeed it can say, "We were there."

Participation is the heart of Eucharist. In the tenth chapter of I Corinthians, before Paul described the institution of the Supper, he speaks of the cup and the bread as our *participation* in the blood and body of Christ (I Corinthians 10:6). The very act of eating makes bread and wine part of us, and we become part of the Lord's life. Participation is also the thrust of the gospel reading. The images used to describe the footwashing in the appointed gospel evoke participation. "If I do not wash you, you have no part of me" (John 13:8). In fact, in the ensuing conversation with Peter, Jesus uses language so evocative of baptism that one may wonder whether the footwashing is not a kind of crypto-initiation. It is even possible to speculate that footwashing never became one of the canonical sacraments, despite the dominical injunction to "wash one another's feet," precisely because it was understood at an early date to duplicate baptism—the washing away of sin and participation in the death and resurrection of Christ.

Thus whether one preaches on the institution of the Eucharist or on the foot-washing, the preacher will be involved in an exposition of the basic sacramental character of Christian liturgy and Christian living. In action as well as word, in the use of material things, such as water, wine and bread, the faithful Christian community continues year by year to participate in the death and resurrection of Christ, and to appropriate the forgiveness of sins and everlasting life, and then to live by them. The power of God, through these sacramental means, makes it possible for the power of past events, supremely those of Holy Week, to be present for those who believe and remember.

Good Friday

Good Friday is the center and climax of Holy Week, and united with Easter forms the focus of the whole Christian year. The scope of preaching on Good Friday will depend, of course, on the nature of the services. It seems appropriate in most situations that the principal service of the day should be the Proper Liturgy at noon, when according to the synoptic gospels Jesus was nailed to the cross and his hours of agony began (Matthew 27:45, Mark 25:33, Luke 23:44). (The Fourth Gospel does not mention the hour, but it says nothing to contradict the synoptic account.)

Parish custom and the desirability of making the Good Friday services accessible to all the congregation may alter this arrangement. In many cases it will be desirable to provide services in the morning or evening, or perhaps both, for those who are unable to come to church during the middle of the day. For this expanded schedule, it would seem practicable to use Morning Prayer in the early morning and Evening Prayer at a convenient hour at the end of the work day. Preaching is not required at the Daily Office. However, especially in churches with a staff of two or more, it would be appropriate to preach a homily about Peter's discipleship and ours, based on John 13:36–38 appointed for the morning, and about Jesus' death and ours, based on John 19:38–42 appointed for evening.

The Three Hours: There has been a long-standing tradition in some Anglican parishes to provide services for the "Three Hours," so that people who wish to do so could watch through the whole time Jesus is said to have hung on the cross. Several liturgical possibilities present themselves for a three-hour service. If Morning and Evening Prayer are to be used as suggested in the previous paragraph, then a three-hour service articulated into three segments and requiring three sermons could be devised as follows:

12n–1pm   The Proper Liturgy and Sermon

1pm–2pm   Litany and Sermon

2pm–3pm   An Order of Worship for Evening and Sermon

If the Daily Office is not to be otherwise used, a second possibility for the Three Hours might be

12n–1pm   Morning Prayer and Sermon

1pm–2pm   Proper Liturgy and Sermon

2pm–3pm   Evening Prayer and Sermon

The use of the Seven Last Words, a series of meditations based on Jesus' words from the cross according the four Gospels, was once popular and not without power. It is not part of the Anglican liturgical tradition, however, at least as this tradition is reflected in its Prayer Books; and it places a heavy burden on the preacher. It sometimes is used as a device to share preaching among a number of speakers, usually with disastrous results.

The Good Friday Gospel: The passion narrative dominates Good Friday, as indeed it should. From very early times John's account has been read. The preacher could approach this lection as he or she approached the Palm Sunday gospel reading, looking at the cross through the eyes of those whose lives touched Jesus' during his last hours. Many of the characters are the same: Judas, Peter, Caiaphas, the maid, Pilate . . . But in John's telling of the story, Pilate's confrontation with Jesus is reflected at length; and we have some new characters: the "disciple whom Jesus loved" and the three Marys—Jesus' mother, and the wife of Clopas, and Mary Magdalene—four who waited with Jesus until he died.

Pilate and Jesus engage in a profound and profoundly Johannine discussion of kingship and truth. The ambiguity of power in relation to justice, and the even greater ambiguity of knowledge in relation to truth, is posed by Pilate's shrugging question, "What is truth?" A meditation on these themes would be a most appropriate use of one of three Good Friday sermons.

One of the striking features of the Fourth Gospel's passion narrative is the note that the title which was nailed to the top of the cross to show the offense for which Jesus was executed was written in Hebrew, Latin and Greek. The preacher might develop a sermon on the lordship of Christ crucified. "God is reigning from the tree," as a sixth-century hymn puts it (*The Hymnal 1982*, no. 162). The love and total commitment measured by the cross express the power and the nature of Christ's lordship, and the three languages point to the three domains in which he rules: Hebrew, the language of religion; Latin, the language of empire; Greek, the language of culture. Do we accept the crucified One as Lord of our religion, our nation, our cultural and intellectual life?

The three Johannine words of Jesus from the cross also merit the preacher's attention: "I thirst," "Woman, behold your son! . . . Behold your mother." "It is finished."

The first of these, "I thirst," is put in homiletical perspective by Cecil Frances Alexander's hymn,

His are the thousand sparkling rills
That from a thousand fountains burst,
And fill with music all the hills;
And yet he says, 'I thirst.'

The selfishness, greed, blindness and ignorance which made Jesus thirst on the cross are factors which still work to produce the hungers, thirsts and needs of poverty-stricken people everywhere. The injustice which crucified the Lord of life contributes to the environmental crisis. Despoiling of nature is part of the world's passion, illuminated by the thirsting of the Son of God.

The second word knits up the relation between his mother and the disciple whom Jesus loved. The two faithful watchers are set together in the love of the dying Christ. This word invites an

Charles P. Price   91

exploration of the new relationship among all Christian disciples, a relationship made possible by the self-giving of the crucified. We are, after all, all beloved disciples. The church is born at the foot of the cross.

The third Johannine word from the cross, "It is finished," permits the preacher to recognize on the one hand the horror of Jesus' agony and the finality of his death, and on the other hand the accomplishment of everything a human being could do to establish the kingdom of God—to die in faith after living in love and obedience. The offering of vinegar "to fulfill the scripture" is an allusion to Psalm 69:23. In this psalm, as in Psalm 22, the suffering of an afflicted person leads to the mighty act of God for our salvation, reversing human disobedience and sin. "As for me, I am afflicted and in pain; your help, O God, will lift me up on high . . . For the Lord listens to the needy, and his prisoners he does not despise" (Psalm 69:31,35). It is regrettable that these verses are not included in the part of the psalm appointed to be read on Good Friday.

Other Lections: The other lections appointed for Good Friday are powerful and apt. The first Old Testament option is the fourth Song of the Servant from Isaiah 52:13–53:12, probably the most famous one. This haunting and beautiful poem introduces, both into the sequence of Isaianic songs and into Holy Week observances, the idea of vicarious suffering. "Surely, he has borne our griefs,/ and carried our sorrows . . . he bore the sin of many,/ and made intercession for the transgressors" (Isaiah 53:4,11). The notes of innocence and non-resistance are there also: ". . . he had done no violence,/ and there was no deceit in his mouth" (v.9). Moreover, the prophet describes the suffering of the servant as a sin-offering (*asham*, v.10), and the prophet promises that the Lord will prevail through this suffering: "the will of the Lord shall prosper in his hand;/ he shall see the fruit of the travail of his soul . . ." (vv.10–11).

When these songs were written, their searching insights pertained to the suffering of an earlier King of Israel, or perhaps to the sufferings of the whole people. They aided generations of Jews to come to terms with the agony of existence. Now they also equip Christian believers, gathered in wonder and sorrow before the cross, to come to terms with this event as God's act for the world's redemption. Christians want to say that the prophet's words, like those of many poets, plumb depths which the writer himself did not fully comprehend.

When the story of Abraham's sacrifice of Isaac (Genesis 22:1–18) is read in Good Friday context, it invites hearers to make a sacrificial interpretation of the cross, though in a way quite different from the fourth Song of the Servant. Its bearing is perhaps even clearer. God demands that true servants of God offer in sacrifice all they hold dear. Only when Abraham showed himself unequivocally willing to offer his only son did God provide a substitute.

It is said that at one of their breakfast table conversations, Martin Luther's wife Katie asked Luther why a loving God could have demanded such a thing. "Why, Katie," Luther is said to have replied, "he did it himself." The cross, considered as the sacrifice of the son of God, reveals the limitless love of God for his creation. Our response is as limitless an offering back to God as we can manage, of our obedient selves and all that we possess.

This same note is sounded also in Psalm 40:1–14:

"Burnt offering and sin-offering you have not required,
   and so I said, 'Behold, I come.
In the roll of the book it is written concerning me,
"I love to do your will, O my God;
   your law is deep in my heart."
                    (Psalm 40:8–9, cf. Hebrews 10:5–7.)

The appointed Epistle, Hebrews 10:1–25, deepens teaching about sacrifice before the passion narrative is read, and so provides a principle of interpretation for an act which, without such perspective, would seem to be unrelieved tragedy and horror. The passage in question is taken from an extended section of Hebrews, chapters 8–10, which explores the meaning of the death and resurrection of Christ as illuminated by the Atonement Day ceremonies of the

Temple. The author knew that the death of Jesus on the cross had in fact completed what was incomplete in the old sacrificial system.

It is important to realize that the author of Hebrews, along with Paul and the New Testament community as a whole, knew by the involvement of their lives with Jesus, by their faith in his living and dying and new life, that their own access to God had been restored. The effects of sin—alienation from God and estrangement from neighbor—had in fact been overcome. Figuratively speaking, the veil of the temple had been torn in two. Where before only the high priest could go into the presence of God once a year, now Christians could, figuratively speaking, come and go freely. Early Christians knew that freedom of access to be a result which the old sacrificial system was supposed to have achieved, but never quite did. Jesus' death produced that result. There is no more "reminder (to God, NB!) of sin year after year" (Hebrews 10:3). In that way Christians have learned that Jesus' death was a sacrifice, in fact the only adequate sacrifice; when they contemplate the cross on Good Friday, it is already with no small understanding of what has been accomplished there.

The practical question is how to arrange the Good Friday readings so that this material from Old Testament, Psalms and the Epistle to the Hebrews can get enough homiletical attention. The sacrificial understanding of the cross which these lections introduce can, of course, always be used to amplify and illuminate the gospel narrative. Yet it might be desirable, by making use of one of the schedules for the Three Hours suggested earlier, to address the Christian understanding of sacrifice directly through the use of some of these texts in one of the independent segments of the service.

The Way of the Cross: The latest edition of *The Book of Occasional Services* (New York: Church Hymnal Corporation, 1991) contains a series of brief devotions entitled The Way of the Cross, based on the Stations of the Cross as used in Roman Catholic and a number of Anglican churches. They consist of the traditional fourteen stations, beginning with "Jesus is condemned to death" and ending with "Jesus is laid in the tomb." Although the Way of the Cross should not replace the Proper Liturgy for Good Friday, it would be appropriate as a Good Friday evening service. The whole sequence would probably be too long for Good Friday morning under most circumstances, but a selection might be manageable. (See above, p. 91.) Although no provision for preaching is made in the rubrics of these devotions, a *brief* meditation after the scriptural material at the beginning of each service could be effective. These meditations might explore the characters of the *dramatis personae*, allowing the hearers to identify their lives in turn with the spiritual crises of each participant in the sacred story.

Holy Saturday

The service on Holy Saturday morning falls between the major efforts of Good Friday and the round of Easter services. A sermon is optional, as the parenthesis in the rubrics indicates: "After the Gospel (and homily) . . ." It will be tempting to take that option. Yet this morning is the one occasion in the Church year when the liturgical anamnesis (which is always complete, to be sure) finds its focus on a dead Jesus entombed on the second day. From one point of view, the commemoration is a blinding contradiction. No wonder there is no Eucharist!

Yet the lesson from Job ("But man dies and is laid low;/ man breathes his last, and where is he?") and the *De Profundis* ("Out of the depths have I called to you, O Lord . . ." Psalm 130:1) provide eloquent texts for exploring the darkness of life and death when there seems to be no hope. A counsel of perfection would indicate a homily on this day, at least in occasional years.

The Great Fifty Days

O. C. Edwards, Jr.

How Not to Preach

In recalling preaching I have heard or heard about during this greatest preaching season of the church's year, it seems that any remarks about how Paschaltide is celebrated homiletically need to begin with negative suggestions before they move on to positive ones. In particular: *Don't act as though Easter were only one day, the opening Sunday in the season!* Such an understanding is clearly contradicted by the Prayer Book's designation of the successive Sundays *of* Easter rather than *after* Easter. A related accomplishment of the 1979 Prayer Book has been to correct the other erroneous impression that the season of Easter ends with the feast of the Ascension. Once again we have the Great Fifty Days celebrated by the early church, this week of weeks when the Body of Christ commemorates the Paschal Mystery that is the cause and shape of our existence.

Indeed, the theme of the resurrection is not exhausted in this season of the church year. Before this annual commemoration was begun, the church was already having a weekly remembrance. Each Sunday is a little Easter, as the Sunday collects for Morning and Evening Prayer, the Saturday collect for Compline, and the proper preface "Of God the Son" for the Lord's Day make clear. This weekly recollection of Easter is strengthened by the similar provisions that make every Friday a little Good Friday.

But even this does not do justice to the paschal character of all liturgical commemoration in the church. In *Liturgy and Education* (New York: Seabury Press, 1965), Massey Shepherd said: "Each single feast renews the fullness and fulfillment of the Feast of feasts, our death and resurrection with Christ" (p. 99). I was reminded of this quotation by my colleague, Leonel Mitchell, in his book *Praying Shapes Believing* (Minneapolis: Winston Press, 1985; p. 14), who also reminded me of this principle in a story he told me once about attending the eucharist on a saint's day at Notre Dame. The celebrant began his homily by saying, "The reason we commemorate Saint (whoever it was) today is that his life was a witness to the Paschal Mystery." The rest of the homily was about the Mystery; nothing more was said about the worthy being remembered. Every Christian celebration is a recalling of Easter. The least we can do is make that our theme throughout the Great Fifty Days.

The next negative admonition is: *Do not waste time trying to prove the scientific or philosophical possibility of the resurrection or trying to reconstruct it historically!* We were called to proclaim the resurrection, not to prove it. To begin with, there is no way that we could establish its historicity. The appearance stories in the gospels cannot be harmonized in such a way that we can say with confidence exactly what happened. In reference to only one detail of such a reconstruction, Raymond Brown once wrote: "To do justice to all the accounts one would have to posit a half dozen angels in various postures inside and outside the tomb" (*Commonweal*, 11/14/67, p. 234). There are times when the work of Christian apologetic must be done from the pulpit, but not now, and never in such a way that the need to prove seems to arise more out of the preacher's own doubt than that of parishioners.

Closely related is the third negative admonition: *Never forget that we are talking about Christian faith in the resurrection rather than a general belief in the immortality of the soul.* The other curate at the time in the city where I served my curacy went in great distress to our suffragan bishop to reveal to him that the rector under whom he served had preached heresy on Easter: he had preached immortality instead of resurrection. The suffragan very calmly began to ask if the rector had said such and such and so and so. The curate (now a bishop himself) had to admit in amazement that the rector had said exactly that. "Well," said the bishop, "that's what he said eighteen years ago when I was his curate and what he's said every Easter since. He always preaches the same sermon." That old priest had a pastoral heart as big as all outdoors, but during his long incumbency his people never heard from him the basic Christian proclamation.

This negative principle leads to another: *Easter sermons should not be devoted to assuring members of the congregation of their own personal survival!* It is Christ's victory over death (and sin) that we celebrate rather than our own. Of course, his makes ours possible, but if the emphasis remains egocentrically on our own desire to escape extinction, we have missed the point. The difficulty here is the same as that with hellfire and brimstone preaching: fear of punishment and hope for reward can never bring about the self-forgetfulness and concern for others that Christ came to bring. Besides, an eternity spent in progressively greater assimilation to the *agape* of God may not seem like much of an escape to the one whose aim is to avoid personal extinction.

What Can Be Proclaimed

It may seem as though most of what one might have said in Eastertide sermons has been eliminated, but with this redressed balance what remains to be proclaimed are the basic affirmations of the Christian religion. To begin with, *Praise God for the Mighty Acts by which the divine purpose is being accomplished!* In the biblical tradition worship always begins with praising God for being who God is and doing what God does. The message of Easter is that the divine purpose in creation has not been, will not be, cannot be frustrated. God's venture in the creation of the human race will achieve its goal. The capacity of human beings to become the holy people of God and to bask in the fellowship of the divine society of the Holy Trinity remains open after every effort of our own self-will and of all the other forces of evil to close it. And this is so because God is always on the alert to make the best of our bad jobs, however expensive the remedy may be in love. Thus the church sings:

> Rejoice now, heavenly hosts and choirs of angels,
> and let your trumpets shout Salvation
> for the victory of our mighty King.

> Rejoice and sing now, all the round earth,
> bright with a glorious splendor,
> for darkness has been vanquished by our eternal King.

The second positive principle has been implied already: *Show how the Easter victory is extended to human beings through the creation of a holy people.* Part of the effect of Christ's death and resurrection is to renew the Israel of God. This is to say, in Schillebeeckx's vocabulary, that the church is the sphere of divine-human encounter, it is the community that exists to have encounter with God. This corporate dimension of salvation is the other side of the negative principle that Easter does not celebrate the individual's escape from death. The New Testament does not know any relation with God that is merely personal; it does not hold forth the possibility that one could have a private "thing" going with God. Rather, relation with God is always mediated through the community of the people of God. This is seen in the Book of Acts, which is an account of the spread of the Spirit-filled community. One comes into relation with God by entering the Spirit-filled community, the community that is the sphere of Divine-human encounter.

This implies the next positive principle: *Never forget that the Great Fifty Days ends with the bestowal of the Holy Spirit at Pentecost.* Thus the Paschal celebration is a time for remembering the Holy Spirit as well as the resurrection. This connection is a helpful correction of a tendency on the part of many Christians towards tritheism, a tendency to act as though one could have a transaction with one of the Persons of the Trinity in which the other two were not involved. But both St. Augustine and St. Thomas Aquinas, probably the two greatest theologians in the history of the church, have reminded us that the only differences between the Persons of the Trinity are differences of relation of origin. Thus one cannot distinguish between the mission and the work of the Son and the Holy Spirit. It is technically incorrect, for instance, to speak of "a personal relation with Jesus" in such a way as to exclude the Father and the Paraclete, or to suggest that the Holy Spirit has done something in one's life independently of the other two Divine Persons. The Great Fifty Days, then, is a Trinitarian celebration in which the Father's will is accomplished in the Son's resurrection and the bestowal of the Holy Spirit.

Growing out of the principles that salvation is made available to us corporately through the church and that the Paschal Mystery involves the gift of the Spirit as well as the resurrection is the principle that *Easter preaching should make it clear that the grace of these events is mediated sacramentally*. At the Easter Vigil the celebrant says, "Through the Paschal mystery, dear friends, we are buried with Christ by Baptism into his death, and raised with him in newness of life." Yet we also speak of baptism as "new birth by water and the Holy Spirit." The first rubric for the baptismal rite confirms this relation by saying: "Holy Baptism is the full initiation by water and the Holy Spirit into Christ's Body the Church." But just as the Passover of the Exodus involved a sacred meal, so does that of the Christians. "Christ our Passover is sacrificed for us; Therefore let us keep the feast!" By the sacred rites of Baptism and Eucharist we are incorporated and reinforced in the Body of Christ, the Spirit-filled community.

All of this emphasis on praising God for the mighty acts of redemption does not mean that Easter preaching is so caught up in doxology that there is no room for the ethical implications of the gospel. Another of my colleagues at Seabury-Western, Timothy Sedgwick, has written a wonderful book called *Sacramental Ethics* (Philadelphia: Fortress Press, 1987) in which he states that all

Christian behavior is a matter of living out the Paschal Mystery of dying and rising with Christ. This principle applies to social as well as personal ethics. Some years ago there appeared a cartoon showing a priest calling on an obviously impoverished young mother in her tenement flat and saying to her, "Remember, we are an Easter people, and Alleluia is our song." His theology was excellent, but his pastoral sense was anesthetized. It is by living out our neighbor love that we manifest what God has accomplished in us through the power of the cross and resurrection.

After dealing seriously with the ethical implications of the Paschal Mystery, one can then *proclaim the hope of life forever with God.* But here again the corporate dimension must be foremost. The issue is not personal escape from eternal punishment into a reward of everlasting blessedness. The Revelation pictures heaven so completely in terms of a liturgical assembly that Massey Shepherd once suggested that the book was a paschal eucharistic rite. While his thesis has not been accepted by many other New Testament scholars, anyone can see how the idea might have occurred to him. Dante, too, imagined the life of heaven to consist of basking in the glory of God and praising it.

"To Father, Son, and Holy Ghost,"
All Heaven broke forth, "Be glory!"—such sweet din,
My sense was drunken to the uttermost;

And all I saw, meseemed to see therein
  A smile of all creation; thus through eye
  And ear I drew the inebriate rapture in.

O joy no tongue can tell! O ecstasy!
  O perfect life fulfilled of love and peace!
  O wealth past want, that ne'er shall fade nor fly!
            (*Paradise*, Canto XXVII,
        Dorothy L. Sayers, *Penguin translation*)

The promise is summed in the words of I John 3:2: "Beloved, we are God's children now; what we will be has not yet been revealed.

What we do know is this: when he is revealed, we will be like him, for we will see him as he is."

The Resources of the Lectionary

After the principles for preaching in the Great Fifty Days have been reviewed, it is possible to look at the biblical passages the church has given to us to preach from during that period. The first thing we note is that the propers for the great feasts remain essentially the same for all three years in our lectionary cycle. At the Easter Vigil, for instance, the epistle is always the passage from Romans about those who are baptized being baptized into the death of Christ, and the gospel is always Matthew's story of the two Marys going to the tomb.

For Easter Day the variation is in the gospel selection. The first reading is always Peter's sermon to the people Cornelius had gathered at Caesarea, which begins with his new insight that God shows no partiality between peoples. The second reading is always the passage from Colossians exhorting that those who are risen with Christ should seek things above. The gospel in year A may be the Matthean passage read at the Vigil or it may be John's account of how first Mary Magdalene and then Peter and the Beloved Disciple go to the empty tomb. The gospel for year B is Mark's "shorter ending," the story of the visit of the women to the tomb with which the earliest manuscripts end. What a strange ending for a gospel: "For they were afraid!" Yet most scholars today are convinced that was Mark's original ending and give interesting if not always unanimous explanations of how the ending could be appropriate. And for year C we hear Luke's account of the visit of the women to the tomb.

All readings for the feast of the Ascension are the same for all three years. The first reading begins with Luke's preface to Theophilus and goes on to recount the ascension forty days after the resurrection. The second reading is a section of Ephesians that refers to Christ as seated at the right hand of power in the heavenly places. The gospel begins with Luke's resurrection appearance to the Twelve after the supper at Emmaus and concludes with the separation of Jesus from the disciples. The reading should include the words left out of some manuscripts: "and was carried up into heaven." It is confusing to think that the same author spoke of an Easter Day ascension in one book and of one forty days later in another, but one of the axioms of text criticism is that "the most difficult reading is to be preferred." Thus preaching on this occasion is an invitation to do one's homework on Lukan theology.

The propers for Pentecost are also the same every year. The first lesson is invariably the story of Pentecost from Acts. The second is the passage from 1 Corinthians that talks about varieties of charismata from the same Spirit. And the gospel is the story of the first resurrection appearance to the disciples in the Fourth Gospel, the one at which Jesus breathes on them, tells them to receive the Holy Spirit, and gives them the power of binding and loosing sins.

The Sundays between these great feasts vary year to year. One thing they have in common, though, is that none of them takes their first lessons from the Hebrew Bible. All come from the Book of Acts and deal in one way or another with the spread of the Spirit-filled community from Jerusalem to Rome (the "ends of the earth"). Yet the readings chosen from Acts are different for each of the three years. In year A they include Peter's sermon at Pentecost, the baptism of more than 3,000 in response, the appointment of the "deacons" (who are never referred to by that title), the split Paul caused at the synagogue at Thessalonica, Paul's speech on Mars Hill at Athens, and Jesus' promise of the Holy Spirit. For year B they tell of Peter's speech in which he says that the authorities crucified Jesus in ignorance, another in which he declares that there is no name under heaven by which we shall be saved other than that of Jesus, the report he makes to the church on that speech, the story of Philip's encounter with the Ethiopian eunuch, the account of the founding of the church at Antioch where "they were first called Christians," and the election of Matthias. The pericopes read in year C recount how the apostles tell the authorities that they must obey God rather than humans, Paul's experience on the Damascus road (the first of the three versions), his preaching in Antioch of Pisidia, the follow-up to that episode, the way that Paul and Barnabas were mistaken for Hermes and

Zeus at Lystra, and the healing of the woman that tradition names as "Thekla." How appropriate it is to have these stories of the triumphant spread of the Spirit-filled community during the Great Fifty Days!

For second lections, each of the three years has its own book from which it does course reading. 1 Peter provides the lessons for year A, a very appropriate choice since many scholars believe that this document started off as a baptismal homily (some even say liturgy!) that was edited to make it an appropriate letter to people who were expecting persecution. Thus it is full of paschal language and touches on many of the principles given above for preaching in Easter. For year B the readings come from 1 John, a letter that Raymond Brown thinks represents a time when "the community of the Beloved Disciple" had suffered the exodus of members with docetic inclinations. The theme of Christian love is presented as it is in few other places in the New Testament. Finally the second lessons during year C are taken from the Revelation. As mentioned above, these are full of the heavenly liturgy and offer a good way to tie in the "already" of Easter with the "not yet" of the Parousia.

The Easter gospels may be a little surprising to anyone who doesn't remember what they are. Instead of coming from the synoptic gospel emphasized each year, they are, for the most part, taken from the Fourth Gospel, in some ways the least paschal of the gospels. John's metaphor of salvation is not the temporal one of the synoptics, "the reign of God," but is the spatial one of the "the world above." Jesus came to the world below to make it possible for men and women to go to the world above. Thus John can treat the lifting up of Christ on the cross as the beginning of his return journey to his home with Father. In some ways resurrection hardly seems necessary except for tying up loose ends with his followers. Yet each of the passages chosen has a wonderful appropriateness when it is considered in its paschal context.

For those who wish to observe the principles listed above for preaching during the Great Fifty Days, the readings appointed for the season offer an inexhaustible treasure. In several lifetimes one could not go through all they have to tell us about the Christian Pasch.

The Sundays after Pentecost

G. Milton Crum, Jr.

PREACHING on the Sundays after Pentecost. It is a time for pentecostal preaching, so let's look at the biblical story of Pentecost as a guide for doing it.

The Pentecost Story

The Pentecost story in Acts 2:1–4 is sometimes treated as if it were a report of a bizarre meteorological phenomenon, but let's approach it here as a story of pentecostal preaching, both then and now.

The story can be read as "dramatic history." Dramatic history differs from history as a mere recitation of facts. Dramatic history dramatizes what happened in order to convey significance and meaning. Events might be compressed or reordered for the sake of focus and intensity.

The story tells of the fulfillment of the day of Pentecost, not a mere chronological fulfillment, but the fulfillment of the meaning of the feast. Pentecost evolved from an agricultural festival to become a day for commemorating the old covenant between God and humanity as established at Mt. Sinai. This old covenant was fulfilled in the new covenant as established by God's speaking through Jesus. In the old, Moses spoke on earth. In the new, Jesus speaks from heaven (Hebrews 12:25).

As the story opens, Jesus had not spoken and the Holy Spirit had not come, but Scripture teaches that people are never without some spirit. If it is not a holy spirit, it will be an unholy, unhealthy spirit (Luke 11:24–26). Some of the unholy spirits which possessed people, then as well as now, were the spirits of condemnation, of worthlessness, of uselessness, and of hopelessness. So we can think of the people in the story as being possessed by such unholy spirits.

> Suddenly there was an *ēchos*,
>> an *ēchos* from heaven,
>> an *ēchos* as being carried along by a strong wind.

I have used the Greek *ēchos* rather than any of the translations because the meaning of the story hangs on how this word is understood. The word can mean "noise" or "sound," but it is also used for the voice of gods speaking. What might St. Luke have had in mind when he used the word?

Luke uses *ēchos* only here and in his Gospel at 4:37. There the word is variously translated as the "report" or "news" or "story" concerning Jesus that went out into every surrounding place. As such, *ēchos* acts as a synonym for *logos*, which Luke uses in two parallel passages, Luke 5:15 and 7:17.

Luke's use of *ēchos* in this way could have been influenced by the fact that contemporary medical writings mentioned medicines for restoring one's *ēchos*, that is, one's speaking voice.

The metaphor of Jesus as the *logos* (word) which God the Source speaks and sends to humans is widely used, particularly in the Fourth Gospel, but Jesus is also called the *ēchos*. In the *Acts of Peter*, Peter asks, "What else is Christ but the Word *(logos)*, the Speaking *(ēchos)* of God?"

Suddenly, there was an *ēchos*. The news about, the story about, the gospel about Jesus was heard. It was heard as an echo in which something which has been heard directly is heard again, wondrously, as the speaking of God.

So the story says that an *ēchos* was heard "from heaven." In Scripture, "heaven" designates the "place" from which God speaks. At Sinai, foreshadowing Pentecost, God said, "I have spoken to you from heaven" (Exodus 20:22). In Luke 3:22, God speaks from heaven at the baptism of Jesus, and Jesus speaks from heaven to Saul on the road to Damascus in Acts 9:3–6. When the *ēchos* of the gospel is heard with authority, an ultimate by-God-it-is-true-for-me authority, it is heard "from heaven."

Not only was the *ēchos* at Pentecost heard "from heaven," it came as if carried by a strong wind. When the gospel is heard with authority, it comes like the wind—not like the noise of wind, but like the power of wind. Cannot gospel images and affirmations penetrate a person with a powerful impact just as wind can?

The word for "wind" used here is also used for the speaking "breath" of God in the Greek Old Testament. So we have a picture of Pentecost as God's breath-wind speaking the *ēchos*-gospel of Jesus with authority and power. It is a faith-picture of the mystery that, through humanly preached words, a word beyond these words can be communicated with sufficient authority and power to affect a person's life.

The story portrays this internal effect of the gospel-*ēchos* by the image of the "tongues of fire." For Jeremiah, God's word was like fire burning in his bones. In James' letter, the word is called a "tongue of fire." John Wesley heard the gospel as an *ēchos* from heaven, and his "heart was strangely warmed."

There was enough gospel to warm the hearts of all, for the tongues of fire were distributed to everyone in the room. When they heard the *ēchos*-gospel with such authority and power that it rested on their minds and hearts like tongues of fire, then they were filled with the Holy Spirit.

Cannot this story, then, be read as dramatic history which sums up the results of innumerable gospel preaching events? Preaching with authority and power can fittingly be called pentecostal preaching. Indeed, if the Pentecost story is read in this way, what might have been some of the content of such preaching by which unholy spirits were cast out and by which persons were filled with a Holy Spirit?

For those possessed by a spirit of condemnation, it could have been a gospel of forgiveness. An image of Jesus dying for our sins, words of forgiveness said by Jesus, the Sacrament of the Body and Blood—such things might well convey an *ēchos* that, by God, a person is really not condemned but forgiven. And, if this *ēchos* is heard as in the Pentecost story, the unholy spirit of condemnation is cast out and a person is filled with the Holy Spirit of mercy.

For those possessed by a spirit of worthlessness, an *ēchos* of by-God worth might be communicated through the image of Jesus as a housewife who searches her house to find coins—lost like us, or through Jesus' explicit affirmations of human worth. When such an *ēchos* penetrates like the wind, the Holy Spirit of a by-God self-esteem will enter.

A person possessed by an unholy spirit of uselessness might need to hear about a Jesus who trusted and used disciples who had really blown it. Or a person paralyzed by an unholy spirit of hopelessness might need a grand vision of God as the Provider and Ruler in whom one can hope for a future.

As the gospel was, or is, preached in many tongues—that is, in its many aspects, idioms, and applications—the Pentecost story was, and is, actualized.

Pentecostal Preaching

From Advent to Pentecost, the lectionary takes worshipers through the Jesus events. Getting through the story of the life and death of Jesus and the feasts which celebrate things he did is often a busy time. Now, on the Sundays after Pentecost, these events can be heard again, less busily. Maybe this time, these things can be heard as an *ēchos*. If so, it is possible that on these Sundays the gospel can be heard more fully, with authority and power sufficient to replace some unholy spirit with some Holy Spirit. But, for such pentecostal preaching to happen, sermon preparation itself needs to be a pentecostal experience also.

In preparing for pentecostal preaching, preachers need to hear old gospel images and affirmations again, as an *ēchos*, with such existential authority and power that some of their unholy spirits are cast out, and they are filled with more Holy Spirit. Then, it may be possible to preach with the "full conviction" that made it possible for Paul to preach the gospel, "not only in word, but also in power and in the Holy Spirit" (1 Thessalonians 1:5).

With the Pentecost story as a paradigm for pentecostal preaching, let's now examine the readings for a Sunday in Pentecost (Proper 3, Year A) for what *ēchos* might be conveyed through them.

In the Isaiah reading, the people of Jerusalem say,
> The Lord has forsaken me;
> my Lord has forgotten me.

So the Lord answers,

> Can a woman forget the infant at her breast,
> or a mother the child of her womb?
> But should even these forget,
> I shall never forget you.
> I have inscribed you on the palms of my hands,

> *or*

> I have written your name on the palms of my hands.

In the First Corinthians reading, Paul describes his bad situation:

> We are in disgrace! To this day . . . we are treated as the
> scum of the earth.

In the Matthew reading, Jesus speaks about being anxious concerning food and clothing and the future.

> A person might know and focus on any of these unholy
> spirits:
> the spirit of feeling forsaken and forgotten by God;
> the spirit of feeling in disgrace;
> the spirit of anxiety.

For now, let's focus on the first one, from Isaiah.

What is it to feel forsaken and forgotten by God? It is easy to say what it means to be forsaken and forgotten by people, but it is more difficult to say what it means in relation to God, is it not?

To say what one means by being forsaken and forgotten by God, one must, as the Ascension Collect says, "ascend in heart and mind." Ascend into heaven? It is to see not only earthly, visible, tangible things; but, with the eyes of faith, with the eyes of imagination, it is to see invisible, intangible, "heavenly" things. It is to see one's visible, earthly world in relation to the invisible, heavenly world of faith images and affirmations. As one becomes like a little child (Matthew 18:3), one can enter this invisible, heavenly "kingdom" of faith-imagination, and it can become more real, more authoritative, and more powerful in one's life than the so-called "real" visible, earthly world.

Forsaken and forgotten by God. What can it mean? The Matthew reading about anxiety offers a clue. Did I once have a faith-image of a God who I believed would always provide me with a way to make it in this world? Now, I suffer unholy anxieties about my job, my income, my future. It is as if the God whom I once trusted has forsaken and forgotten me, and I am up against a cold, uncaring, competitive process.

Even in such an anxious spirit, can I hear an *ēchos* through the words from Isaiah? Can my faith-imagination once again see the invisible God who loves me as a Heavenly Mother whose love exceeds that of earthly mothers? Can I see myself, my name, inscribed on the palm of God's hands? Can I trust that, by God, no matter what, a way and the wherewithal to live can be found? Can the Holy Spirit of trust become strong enough to crowd out at least some of the unholy spirit of anxiety? If any of this is so, pentecostal preparation for pentecostal preaching is taking place.

Another clue to meanings of feeling forsaken and forgotten by God is the context of the Isaiah reading. The people were in exile. Exiles are nobodies in a foreign land, and exile is a lonely place to be.

The feeling of being a nobody: good for nothing, insignificant, a failure—not so much on the human level but on a cosmic, ultimate level. Even when I am somebody in the eyes of people, I can feel like a nobody in cosmic terms, in the big picture, in the final analysis, the whole scheme of things. In faith-image terms, it is like being such a nobody in the eyes of God that God has not only forsaken me but forgotten me as if I did not even exist.

A corollary of feeling like a cosmic nobody is the feeling of cosmic loneliness. Even when a person is snug in the womb of human closeness, an unholy spirit of cosmic loneliness can attack. Humanly speaking, we are alone inside our skins; and, cosmically speaking, we can feel alone, forsaken and forgotten by God, possessed by an unholy spirit of loneliness.

But, even then, can you not hear an *echos* of God, as the Heavenly Mother portrayed by Isaiah, saying,

I have not forsaken you.
I have not forgotten you.
I am with you.
I hear what you feel, and I understand.
I am a Nobody in Jesus on the Cross.
I am in your Lonely Place with you.

No matter what you may feel,
    I will never forsake you.
I have inscribed you on the palms of my hands.
I have not only written your name;
    I have drawn your picture.

I will never forsake you.
I will be with you.
I will be your Friend,
    a Friend who knows you completely,
    a Friend who loves and honors you just the way you
        are,
    a Friend who will embrace you and never let you go,
    a Friend who dwells in your heart and mind.

Maybe you can also hear God say,

You are never a Nobody to me.
You are Somebody Special.

G. Milton Crum, Jr.

You are unique, one of a kind, incomparable,
    irreplaceable, a collector's item.
If there were a price tag on you,
    it would be in the shape of the Cross,
    and the price would be written in Jesus' blood.

In your faith-imagination, can't you feel God as your Friend, present with you right now? Can't you feel God's embrace, almost as if it were physical? Can't you hear these by God images and affirmations with such authority and power that they burn in you? Can't you feel the Holy Spirit of God's Presence and of your by God worth and identity?

Can't such a Holy Spirit cast out unholy spirits like the spirits of anxiety, loneliness, and feeling like a nobody? Can't such images and affirmations cast out the unholy spirit of excessive dependence on other people to provide the presence and friendship which only faith can give as well as the unholy spirit of anger toward people when they don't fulfill your dependence?

If any of this happens, you are engaged in pentecostal preparation for pentecostal preaching.

When the preparation has been pentecostal, the preaching can describe being possessed with an unholy spirit with such empathy and authenticity that others who suffer it will be enabled to acknowledge, "That's me also." Then the images and affirmations, which the preacher has received, can be offered so that others might see and hear them in their faith-imaginations. It may be that through the preacher's words, an *ēchos* will be conveyed to at least one listener which is similar to the one received by the preacher, and it may be that some unholy spirits will be crowded out, at least a little bit, by Holy Spirits. If so, the sermon will have become a pentecostal event.

The Pentecost Story and Pentecostal Preaching

The biblical story of Pentecost compresses the results of many sermons into one dramatic event. It is unlikely that any one sermon will accomplish such spectacular results. But the ordinary preaching of the ordinary time of the Sundays after Pentecost can at least strengthen faith-images and faith-affirmations, and do not our bottom line faith images and affirmations generate the spirits by which we live? And do not the spirits by which we live designate the way we live?

Thus, it just might be, if a person wanted to communicate the impact of thousands of ordinary pentecostal sermons, it could be done by telling a dramatic story of one spectacular pentecostal event. Through thousands of sermons to thousands of people, an *ēchos* of the gospel of God was heard with such authority that it seemed to come from heaven and with such power that it seemed to be carried along by a strong wind. The *ēchos* that each person heard so burned in each heart and mind that unholy, unhealthy spirits were crowded out by more healthy holy spirits. Faith images and affirmations became so real and full in people that they lived by them, and they communicated them to other people in idioms and by actions they could understand.

At times the preaching process can seem futile, because faith images and affirmations are so quickly overshadowed by destructive images and affirmations. When this happens, people—including the preachers—act accordingly. At such times, the story of Pentecost serves not only as a story of what *has* happened but as a story to inspirit the preacher with hope for what *can* happen through ordinary pentecostal preaching.

Pentecost and Trinity

For over four centuries, the Anglican tradition spoke of the Sundays after Trinity rather than after Pentecost. In a sense, they still are, because pentecostal preaching is not only Holy Spirit preaching but Trinitarian preaching. It is God the Source/the Father/the Mother who speaks and sends Jesus, the Son/the Word/the *ēchos*; and the Holy Spirit proceeds from the Son when His Gospel-*ēchos* is heard with authority and power.

All preaching cannot properly be called gospel preaching, because some preaching is merely law without gospel images and

G. Milton Crum, Jr.   113 affirmations which might enable a person to obey, and some preaching remains on earth and never enters the "kingdom" of faith-imagination. But all gospel preaching can be called evangelical preaching, because the word "evangel" is a synonym for the word "gospel," both of which mean the "good news" of God. And all gospel preaching can be called pentecostal preaching even if the term Holy Spirit is never used; for when the gospel is preached and heard faithfully, the Holy Spirit is at work as in the Pentecost story.

Special
Times, Persons, and Places

Preaching on Holy Days

H. Boone Porter

As THE SEASONS OF THE CHURCH YEAR and then the numbered Sundays after Pentecost move on their stately annual round, other days stand outside this grand cycle. These occasions commemorate saints and Christian heroes and a few special events and are fixed in the calendar with little or no reference to seasons or sequences of Sundays. Because they generally occur outside of any framework provided by preceding or succeeding days, and because members of the congregation may have little idea of who or what is being commemorated, the task of the preacher is an important one requiring careful preparation, especially when it must be accomplished in a brief address of a few sentences.

Feasts of Our Lord

Among the fixed holy days, some are in the Christmas-Epiphany sequence and are considered elsewhere in this book. Several others occur at intervals during the year, each with a distinct character—such as the Presentation, Annunciation, Visitation, and Holy Cross.

These have each become associated with a wealth of theological and devotional meaning. Because this full range of significance can hardly ever be contained in the collect and readings of one service, it is recommended that, before preparing a sermon for these occasions, the preacher read the entire proper for the feast (including the eve) for both the Daily Office and the Eucharist.

Because they stand outside the narrative flow of the church year, these observances encourage reflection on the considerable implications of the events they celebrate. The various feasts of the Incarnation, for example, give the preacher the opportunity to say things not said at Christmas. In a similar way, Holy Cross Day, half a year from Good Friday, renews and deepens our awareness of the atonement.

Keeping Other Feasts

Most of our fixed holy days commemorate holy people, and such occasions will receive most of our attention in this chapter. These holy days put before us examples of heroism and faith from the earliest Christian times down to the present century, and geographically they reflect a wide diversity of languages, peoples, and nations. Surely so great a cloud of witnesses should be a powerful inspiration to us, both in our worship and in our lives in the world. It is the task of the preacher to help make this happen.

The question then arises as to when such preaching can take place. First, there are the so-called "Red Letter Days," commemorating mostly apostles, evangelists, and other persons or events mentioned in scripture. In the past, in an ordinary year, one or two of the "Red Letter Days" displaced a Sunday and provided obvious opportunity for pertinent preaching. Today this is minimally the case. Secondly, there are the lesser holy days. Although such days were traditionally listed in the calendars printed in other Anglican Prayer Books, they did not enter our official American calendar until the present edition of our Book of Common Prayer came into use—although many parishes had in fact been observing these days long before.

Since most of the fixed holy days are concerned with saints, we will consider in this chapter the broad topic of preaching on saints. This will involve both the infrequent opportunities to do so on Sunday, when a full-length sermon is called for, and the very frequent opportunities to deliver a short homily about saints on weekdays. We will also call attention to some additional opportunities for such sermons on an occasional Sunday. Since the saints and heroes of the Christian faith are an important part of the Church's heritage, we hope that preachers will plan ahead for such sermons at least a few times each year.

First, let us consider the "Red Letter Days" and the opportunities to preach on saints on Sundays. First and foremost, there is the major feast of All Saints. It is assumed that most parishes will wish to take advantage of the rubrical permission to observe this feast on the Sunday following November 1 (BCP, p. 15). Its importance is enhanced by its being one of the days especially appropriate for public baptism (BCP, p. 312). The succession of Halloween (All Hallows' Eve), November 1, All Souls' Day, and the following Sunday provide the buildup for a true feast, an occasion of festivity for individuals and households as well as the parish as a whole. Since All Saints' Day includes this entire range of celebration, a wide variety of approaches is open to the preacher. Especially when there are baptisms, incorporation into the communion of saints will of course be touched on; and even when there are none, this theme can always be linked with the Renewal of Baptismal Vows on this day (BCP, p. 312).

Then there is the patronal feast, or the feast of the title of a church. During most of the year, it may again be transferred to a (BCP, p. 16). This too can be a genuinely festive occasion with a suitably full sermon. It is also worth noting that certain saints enjoy multiple opportunities for celebration. Churches dedicated to St. Peter or St. Paul, for example, can observe one feast in January and another in June. Similarly, those dedicated to our Lord's Mother may observe Mary Day in August as well as one or more of the other feasts associated with her. It is also important to celebrate the connections between parish dedications and the periodic appearance of certain saints in the regular Sunday calendar. In churches named for him, John the Baptist should receive attention not only on his feast in June but also in mid-Advent and on the First Sunday after the Epiphany. Similarly, a church dedicated to St. Thomas may well find the Second Sunday of Easter a more promising time for parish celebration than his appointed feast four days before Christmas.

Some saints have patronal feasts in Advent, Lent, or Easter Season, when transfer to a Sunday is not allowed, and might (in Advent or Lent) be unsuitable anyhow. We would suggest that such churches, with the bishop's consent, declare that their annual observance be transferred in the future to some agreeable time in the late Spring or Fall, when it can truly be a fiesta. In many cases, a church was not actually dedicated or consecrated on its patronal feast, but at some other time. This anniversary may be kept each year, governed by the same rubrics as a patronal feast (BCP, p. 16) and offering comparable opportunities for a sermon related to the saint.

Churches whose dedications do not correspond precisely to any of the holy days in the calendar can often find appropriate occasions to celebrate. Thus Calvary Churches might claim Holy Cross Day, since Good Friday hardly lends itself to festivity. Parishes and hospitals named for the Good Samaritan could fittingly celebrate the feast of St. Luke, both as the evangelist recounting the parable and as the patron of healing. Churches of Our Savior would enjoy a wide range of choices but might well focus on the Transfiguration, an event celebrated both on August 6 and on every Last Sunday after the Epiphany.

It has not been widely noticed that the readings from Acts during the Great Fifty Days give good exposure in different years to such New Testament figures as Stephen, Philip, Barnabas, and others. At least once during this joyful season, a saint can be preached about and a pertinent hymn or two used. As the *Lesser Feasts and Fasts* notes, "the triumphs of the saints are a continuation and manifestation of the Paschal victory of Christ" (1991 ed., p. 56), and it is desirable for the preacher to affirm this truth.

Deserving comparable attention is the rarely noticed rubric (BCP, p. 16) permitting *some* of the proper of the "Feasts of Our Lord and all other Major Feasts" to be used on a Sunday during the numbered weeks after the Epiphany and after Pentecost. This permission opens the gate to the virtual observance of such a day, seeing that usually only one or two of the festal readings would be related to the sermon in any case.

We come at last to the ordinary observance of a saint's day during the week. For pastoral reasons such a day may be transferred to the most convenient day in the week (BCP, p. 17). In most cases, the weekday congregation will be small, and hymns will not be sung. Yet a five-minute homily can be delivered to good effect. Such a brief address requires care and thoughtful preparation. The preacher cannot waste time with rambling comments and observations. Nor can one say everything that might be said! Strong points may be made regarding those apostles about whom scripture and tradition are ample. More general reflections about the apostolic mission or the communion of saints can be saved for the days of those apostles about whom we know little more than a name.

The lesser holy days are numerous, and they will frequently come up, whether a parish has one, two, or six weekday celebrations. Their observance will normally impinge strongly only upon the Holy Eucharist, though their collects will customarily be used as the Collect of the Day in the Daily Office. Time for preaching on these occasions will probably be limited except perhaps for two or three of those figures each year (e.g. Francis of Assisi, Absalom Jones, Nicholas of Myra) to whom a fuller observance may be accorded.

For many clergy, the homiletic practice on holy days during the week is simply to read the one-page commentary from *Lesser Feasts and Fasts*. While it must be acknowledged that this resource provides a most helpful synopsis of the life and teaching of persons being commemorated, such reading is not the same as preaching. A sermon, even the briefest, should take account of the congregation (a small group of weekday worshippers is often well-known to the priest), the circumstances of the parish or place, and the time within which we live. *Lesser Feasts and Fasts* does not pretend to relate to any such pastoral considerations, but it usually provides enough information for the preacher to make such connections. In five minutes one cannot explore all the historical or contemporary implications of a certain person or issue, but a short homily can offer one's hearers at least some point of correlation between their own lives and the faithful witness being remembered.

What Does Such a Sermon Contain?

Normally a sermon should develop out of or somehow relate to the scripture readings of the day. In the case of New Testament events such as the Transfiguration, or New Testament figures such as Paul, the Bible passages give us plenty with which to start. With several of the apostles, however, we find only a name among the list of the Twelve. Among the post-biblical saints there are dozens of whom there can be no possible scriptural mention. What about these cases?

The appointed biblical passages may indeed be interesting and stimulating, but exegesis is not the preacher's primary task on these days. Holy days do not exist simply to provide a means of introducing variety in the lectionary. Our purpose on these days is to celebrate the victories of Christ in and through the lives and deaths of his faithful servants. The compilers of the lectionary have simply tried to choose passages which would orchestrate and endorse the acts and words of the holy men and women who are held up before us on these days.

It is, after all, the particular holy life—and often the holy death—of identifiable individuals or groups of individuals which we celebrate to the extent that our information and understanding permit. We are not just applauding sanctity in general or martyrdom in general. For this reason a few anecdotes or quotations (of the kind provided in *Lesser Feasts and Fasts*) can be helpful: they affirm the central incarnational features of our faith and practice by making the celebration specific and concrete.

At the same time, such details make a saint, who perhaps lived many centuries ago, closer to us. Some of them faced problems remarkably like our own; some had the same weaknesses we have. Although a saint may have lived long ago and far away, we should leave this commemoration feeling that this is a saint of our Church, part of our heritage, still impinging on our life.

One of the realities we cannot overlook is the matter of martyrdom. Most of the early saints are believed to have died for the faith. We must not forget that men, women, and children really did face "the tyrant's brandished steel, the lion's gory mane" (*The Hymnal 1940*, no. 549). When we are confronted with the fact of martyrdom, whether ancient or modern, our minds can see things with new intensity and clarity. The martyrs knew with searing insight what the Holy Eucharist was all about, for they too surrendered their flesh and blood. When we receive the holy sacrament at the altar, we are united not only with Christ in his sacrifice but also with the whole company of faithful servants who are part of his mystical body in heaven and on earth.

Another impediment to identification with the saints can be a sense of distance from their times and places. To counter this aura of strangeness, a short sermon, or part of a longer one, can sometimes be based on the city or region within which a holy person lived. Such place names as Iona, Lindisfarne, Tours, or Edessa may mean nothing to the majority of worshipers, but the preacher can find sufficient material in encyclopedias or other reference works to invest them with considerable interest. Some distant regions, such as Egypt or Armenia, have received contemporary attention in the press, and the average worshiper will often be interested to learn how the Christian Church has been connected with such places. Geographic location gives specificity to the commemoration of a saint: that the setting is a real place helps us to appreciate that they were real people. Occasionally the preacher may have visited the place where a saint lived and can describe an impressive cathedral, abbey, or shrine there. So much the better, but one must beware of the temptation to indulge in unduly lengthy personal anecdotes. A detailed account on January 13 of a wonderful dinner you were once served in Poitiers may not be appreciated by worshipers who have given up their lunch in order to attend a noonday service!

Often the apostles as well as some of the more popular post-biblical saints may be depicted in a stained glass window, or a reredos, or in other artwork in the church. In such cases the preacher can allude to the representation and may even invite a small congregation to move to the place where they can appreciate it best. Frequently some part of the church is adorned with shields of the apostles or other saints, and their iconography can provide a helpful point of departure for a homily. Even when such ornaments are lacking in a particular building, a preacher may wish to use a large reproduction of a painting, statue, or icon of the saint. Discretion is needed, however. Not every depiction is appropriate for such purposes. The opulent vestments of renaissance prelates with which the Old Masters clothed early Church fathers hardly convey an accurate or helpful impression to worshipers. It is also important that such use of artwork serve as a means toward engaging people in a greater appreciation of the saint rather than simply expanding their cultural acumen.

Hymns are another art form through which we have contact with our ancestors in the faith. The words of many hymns in *The Hymnal 1982* were written by figures in our calendar. Even at a weekday service with no singing, the preacher can ask worshippers to turn to a particular hymn which can illustrate the life and work of the person being remembered on that day. This is especially helpful for persons relatively new to our calendar, such as Ephrem of Edessa (June 10), whose fertile and imaginative style is well represented by hymn 443. In much the same way, hymn 649/650 gives us an aspect of the piety associated with Bernard of Clairvaux (August 20), and various hymns (382, 402/403, 487, 592) convey something of the remarkable spirit of George Herbert (February 27).

A question which is often asked and which preachers occasionally attempt to answer is whether insertion into the calendar of the Prayer Book constitutes canonization. Are all the people listed there to be given the formal title "Saint"? We would suggest that insertion in the calendar is akin to canonization but not quite identical. Many figures in the calendar, including some recent additions, are men and women who have been accorded the title of Saint for centuries. In other cases, it seems wise to allow time and the popular usage of the Church to decide. In the meantime, they can be referred to as Christian heroes, as worthies, as saintly men and women. The title "Blessed" can be prefixed to their names on occasion, if the preacher believes such a title is appropriate. For example, we now generally and very acceptably accord the title "Saint" to Julian of Norwich (May 8) although no earlier beatification or canonization is known to have occurred.

The Saints as Companions, Examples, and Intercessors

For many people, including some very devout folk who attend weekday services, life in general and religion in particular have become a lonely business. It is difficult to go on alone, day after day. The holy saints and angels have been given to us as invisible friends and companions, to encourage us, to cheer us, to teach us, and to pray for us. It is this fellowship of love, made possible by the Holy Spirit, that we seek to make present and recognizable when we gather at the table of life on these days. We may be a small or a large congregation, but we worship "with angels and archangels, and with all the company of heaven," and in that fellowship we find a foretaste of the heavenly kingdom.

Many of the collects for saints' days in the Prayer Book speak of the *example* which saints offer us. This is not a simple matter, and the preacher may seek to discuss it from time to time. Many saints accomplished deeds or wrote or uttered words which we cannot emulate. Some had exceptional gifts which many of us simply do not have. Only in rare cases can we directly and literally do what they did. On the other hand, within the company of God's holy ones, we find here and there a personal hero, an archetypal figure if one will, whose words or deeds, or perhaps whose visual image, may implant themselves deeply in our hearts. Such a one can again and again stir us, draw us, and indeed be a channel of strength and power to us as we pursue the Christian path.

What about the prayers of the saints? In medieval Europe, and still today in some areas, the prayers of the saints for us, and the direct benefits of such prayers to us, have been exaggerated to the point that the saints, rather than Jesus Christ our great High Priest, have been seen as the primary mediators between God and his people. Such exaggeration is not acceptable and must not be encouraged. Yet this does not mean that the saints do not pray, or that we may not seek their prayers. If we ask earthly friends and relatives to pray for us, may we not ask the same of the blessed ones, who have been made our friends and relatives in the holy family of God by the power of the Holy Spirit? Our Prayer Book speaks of a "fellowship of love and prayer" upholding us (pp. 199, 250, 395, 489, 504). Let it indeed be so.

An Abundance of Opportunities

Putting it all together, there are many ways to preach about a saintly person. Where pertinent, the biblical readings, local circumstances, world events, or some personal experience or anecdote can provide a starting point. On a weekday, when time is usually severely limited, one must then move on quickly to the one or two things that seem most fitting to say about the person being commemorated, and then close. The homily may end with something directly applicable to the local scene, or perhaps with a dramatic climax, such as an account of the saint's martyrdom. The long-term strategy, the conveyance of the whole picture of our Lord's Mother and all the saints within the working of the household of God, cannot be achieved in one sermon—and should not be attempted. The contents of many short, well-prepared homilies can add up, however, to a powerful message. In that broad message we see the saints and saintly heroes as those who took Jesus at his word and really did what he said, those who showed what the Holy Spirit can do with a human life, those who showed that the Gospel is indeed true. They all, whether martyrs or not, in some way bore the cross. They all forsook our worldly goals of money, prestige, and power. They all stretch out invisible hands to us, to beckon us, uphold us, and draw us to follow them in that great procession which will end only when we ascend the steps of that beloved and sacred City and ourselves behold the glory of God in the face of Jesus Christ.

Preaching at Marriages

William H. Hethcock

UNTIL RECENT YEARS marriage homilies were infrequent in the Episcopal Church. Two significant developments are underway which call for reconsideration of preaching at marriages.

First, the current renewal of preaching begun in the seventies is encouraging clergy to consider sermons a more important component of worship than before. We have more information on how people listen and hear. Literature on preaching abounds and supports successful experimentation and increased skill among preachers. Preaching's questioning fifties and doubtful sixties have passed, and the importance and integrity of the pulpit are being restored. The sermon has come forth today with a more vital place in liturgical worship and congregational life.

Second, whereas some clergy had previously preached at marriages only on their own initiative, the 1979 Book of Common Prayer now provides for a homily. The marriage rite is prepared to be used either by itself, at which time a sermon is optional, or as the Word of God portion of the Eucharistic liturgy, when preaching seems more strongly recommended.

Another consideration affecting whether to preach at a marriage is the fact that the congregation at a wedding represents a rare homiletical opportunity. People with no Church relationship are almost always present. Frequently the one member of the bridal couple who is a member of the parish has only a peripheral relationship. Some who are present may actually hold the Church in contempt based on hearsay or on unfortunate experiences which support their disdain. A wise preacher who crafts an appropriate sermon may not give a remarkable message there and then, but a word may be planted that comes to fruition years later. This is an opportunity not to be missed. An English vicar writes:

> In spite of the difficulty of the undertaking the minister has a duty before God to preach . . . A sermon at the wedding will liturgically undergird the concept of the family which lies, according to the Bible, near to the heart of God's purpose for the whole world of human relationships. In addition it will point to the great resource, for cementing the bond between a man and a woman, in the good news of Jesus Christ and his self-giving love. The sermon, in other words addresses the whole congregation in proclamation of the good news of God's institution of marriage, its foundations, its purpose, and its responsibilities.[1]

How Our Understanding of Marriage Developed

Our present-day understanding of marriage has evolved over the centuries. The preacher needs to be as informed as possible about these developments. The story begins with the scriptural tradition.

On the one hand, the people of Israel themselves practiced marriage and celebrated the wedding in much the same way as their neighbors who did not know Yahweh. Marriage involved no priest, and there was no visit to the temple. At the proper time two families arranged for their son and daughter to be married so that the family and religious traditions of the people might be continued. But the unique insight of the Hebrews was that Yahweh was the Creator, and the marriage relationship became sacred as it participated in that creation. The operative love in marriage was *hesed*, the steadfast love of God, God's loyal love which flowed unconditionally upon the people. Husband and wife were charged to live that love in their relationship, a covenant not unlike the covenant between God and Israel.

Within the Old Testament, the understanding of human sexuality and marriage deepened under the influence of two leading Old Testament convictions: that creation is good, and that God's covenant with his people sets the standard for all relationships within the covenant, including the relationship between husbands and wives.[2]

The New Testament practice built upon these Hebrew foundations. Marriages continued to be arranged between families. Local customs endured. The man and the woman were their own ministers in this act of covenant-making. The operative love was *agape,* the highest kind of mutual regard and selflessness, love like that God shows for humankind in the person and work of Jesus Christ.

There can be no mistake that the model for Christians of love in marriage is Christ's total self-giving—his *agape.* When Christians try to understand the implications of Christ's life for their lives, they realize that his steadfast love for his church involves, in the case of marriage, the complete loyalty of the man to the woman, and of the woman to the man, for life.[3]

Love and Marriage

Modern couples presenting themselves for marraige are more aware of romantic love than of the *hesed* and *agape* spoken of in scripture. During the Renaissance, Western civilization replaced arranged marriages with marriages by consent between couples drawn together in romantic love, a more personal relationship than arranged marriages had implied. There is nothing new about romantic love, however; it is as old as humankind. In many cultures of the world, and not infrequently among Christians, it has been experienced and sanctioned outside marriage. "It is only recently that love in this sense has come to be regarded as a structural principle of married life."[4]

The ambiguity of the word "love" reminds the preacher of a

central prevailing concern at most marriages, especially those of very young people. The couple is likely not to understand that "love" as it is used in scripture and liturgy has a much more profound meaning than their experience in the world has provided them. They are unaware that the strong feelings drawing them together already occur on more than one level. They need to know that their promise is to love with *agape*, which is accomplished through an act of their wills, sacred in intent and practice; and that taking vows in the light of *agape* means an intent to remain loyal to each other even when romantic love wavers and difficult times prevail. The sermon needs to accomplish a difficult task—bringing this nature of *agape* into focus for everyone without discounting the place of romantic love. If this proclamation is sound and poignant, it will cut through the tendency at weddings to romanticize and over-sentimentalize.

For Whom Is the Sermon Preached?

The preacher must have clearly in mind to whom the sermon is addressed. The temptation will be to speak only to the couple being married, a sermon assuredly easier to craft. The preacher will doubtless be praised for sage advice painstakingly given to a couple about to enter the big risk of life together, but a promising opportunity will have been missed. The sermon is best designed like a sermon at an ordination or the baptism of an adult. It addresses first the whole congregation but toward the end narrows to focus upon the principals, here the couple who will be married. Composing a sermon with this kind of shape presents a real but not insurmountable structural challenge.

The sermon must reflect the preacher's awareness of the variety of life situations among those seeking marriage today. Some couples will have postponed marriage to a later age, which means that their experience in life is more mature. The elderly, who in recent decades might have remained single, today seek to be married for their remaining years. Couples in which one or both parties have canonical permission for a second marriage will present a special circumstance. When the sermon speaks of the indissolubility of

PREACHING AT MARRIAGES

marriage, it must do so without condemnation of painful past failures for which forgiveness and reconciliation have been gained. Children of the persons being married may be in the congregation. We cannot ignore their presence or offend their sensitivities. Well-meaning parents whose marriage plans seek the well-being of their children as well as their own may find that, despite their good intentions, this new relationship is offensive and troublesome to their children.

The congregation includes men and women struggling to make their own marriages survive. Some of them may be strengthened by the words of the sermon, but they may be damaged by the seemingly easy solution of those who have dissolved a marriage and then enter another one with apparent guiltlessness and ecclesial blessing. Also present are single persons for whom marriage has never been an appropriate alternative. The preacher must avoid implying that marriage is "the next step" in the normal life of people moving from school to the workplace, or that those who do not marry are incomplete or lacking. The young singles in the congregation need to know the difference between "wedding" and "marriage," especially if their romantic longing for a mate tempts them to place an end to loneliness above the pledge to a life-long commitment. On the other hand, some of those young people may see their friends suffering from difficult marriages or painful break-ups; they may be avoiding marriage with doubt and fear about their own capacity to form a lasting relationship. Everyone will hear the sermon from a different perspective, but the preacher must be aware of those perspectives before the sermon is begun.

Connecting the Rite and the Sermon

As the canons require, the priest will have spent some time with the couple in preparation for their marriage. In some instances, several couples may have attended the same sessions, but even then the priest does well to spend private time with each couple leading them to consider special issues or components in their relationship. The priest should explain that there will be a sermon, and he or she should make sure that provisions are made for everyone to sit not only during the preaching, but during the psalm and scripture reading as well. These arrangements will also need to be explained to the wedding party at the rehearsal so that everyone can take their seats easily. The congregation will be uncomfortable and inattentive during the sermon if the wedding party remains standing or appears conspicuously confused and ill at ease.

During their preparation, the couple will have been acquainted with the marriage rite and what it means so that they are comfortable with the words and intent of the service. Conversation about the liturgy will help inform the priest of what is important for the couple. While it is clear that the clergy will respect all confidences and private discussions, the sermon might recall to the couple things that were significant for them in the preparation. The sermon may accentuate portions of the service special to them, at the same time drawing the attention of the congregation to the liturgy about to take place. When the sermon's words recur in the liturgy, the people will be reminded of the preacher's message and the liturgy will be better understood.

Especially important is the language of the vows, prayers, and blessings, particularly such phrases as "in faithfulness and patience, in wisdom and true godliness" (BCP, p. 431). The words of the prayers are remarkably down to earth and human. "Give them grace *when* they hurt each other" is realistic; the prayer does not say *"if* they hurt each other." If the longer blessing is chosen, the sermon may prepare the people to notice its comprehensive cadences: "Bless them in their work and in their companionship; in their sleeping and in their waking; in their joys and in their sorrows; in their life and in their death" (BCP, p. 430). The preacher may point out that this is not an ancient ritual repeated for tradition's sake; it is a practical liturgy related to what life is like in both its beauty and its mundane and daily routine.

Considering where the sermon occurs in the liturgy, anticipating in the sermon what is yet to come may be easier than reminding hearers of what has already been said. Although it precedes the sermon, the preacher should not overlook the opening address informing the congregation of what the Church proclaims the

132   PREACHING AT MARRIAGES

purpose of marriage to be. These three components—"mutual joy," "the help and comfort given one another," and "when it is God's will for the procreation of children" (BCP, p. 423)—will have been a part of the priest's instruction and preparation of the couple. There may be some occasions when couples or congregations will especially appreciate a sermon based on these words.

The sermon may recall what the couple's preparation will have included on how a marriage takes place and its sacramental nature. Theologian Owen C. Thomas explains:

> The matter of marriage varies in different cultures, but in the Prayer Book it is the joining of hands and the giving of a ring or rings. The form is the exchanging of vows in the presence of witnesses. The minister is the couple themselves. The blessing by a bishop or priest is not necessary to the sacrament. The "inward and spiritual grace" is the gift of the Holy Spirit to enable the couple to keep their vows.[5]

There is a sense in which the marriage covenant begins when a spark of love starts to grow and flourish between the man and the woman. The love of an engaged couple "is not outside God's influence." But the sacrament is brought to fruition when the couple exchanges vows publicly and in the presence of the witnessing Church. By asserting that when two persons come together their marriage is a sacrament, "we are implying that God himself *does* something, and gives us a tangible proof of his divine action."[6]

The Marriage Sermon and Scripture

As in all preaching, the priest will do well to ground the sermon in scripture. This may be especially important at a marriage. A sermon not scripturally based will sound like more of the abundant advice-giving any marrying couple will already have endured. The authority of the sermon must come from scripture rather than the wisdom of the preacher. The truth is, however, that since the marriage rite has a form and function today that it did not have in the first century, we err if we assume that a reference to marriage in the biblical text is immediately related to what is happening in our rite.

> If we confine the gospel message about Christian marriage to the handful of texts that refer directly to it, we are distorting it inexcusably. For the theology of Christian marriage the most important Gospel texts are not those that refer to marriage but those that refer to the sacrificial love of Jesus, and to the kind of love he therefore demands from his followers.[7]

The larger subject of Christ's demonstrated *agape* is the biblical reference pertaining to the marriage covenant. In every instance the predisposition of the congregation to understand "love" in its romantic sense must be addressed. The word "love" as it appears in the readings must be made clear. It is at best difficult to make this point; at worst it will not be heard among marginal Christians. Regardless of how limited the priest may see his or her chances to speak this message effectively to a given congregation, the preacher must remember what the central message of *agape* really is.

Genesis 2:4–9,15–24 is helpful here. This reading about the creation of Adam and Eve leads to the verse which says, "Therefore a man leaves his father and mother and clings to his wife, and they become one flesh" (NRSV). A popular misunderstanding in the contemporary culture may be that "one flesh" means a loss of individual identity, will, and personality. Rather, "one flesh" refers to one intention, shown by the two persons' taking similar vows to be joined in one kind of love, *hesed* or *agape.*

Colossians 3:12–17 speaks of the climate created when *agape* prevails: "Above all, clothe yourselves with love, which binds everything together in perfect harmony." Paul enumerates characteristics which benefit an intimate loving relationship: "compassion, kindness, humility, meekness, and patience."

The gospels present a greater problem for the expository preacher. The beatitudes are a homiletical obstacle in any event. The parable of building a house upon a rock can be somewhat obscure at a marriage. One does not merely build a house in a

PREACHING AT MARRIAGES

marriage; one *loves.* The house-building image may imply to some that marriage grows stronger through trying harder rather than through loving faithfully. Better is John 15:9–12, which makes a clearer statement. "As the Father has loved me, so I have loved you . . . I have said these things to you so that my joy may be in you, and that your joy may be complete." The intimate language of *agape* which Jesus uses in addressing his disciples is related to the intimate love between a husband and a wife. This love is what is spoken of when we vow "to love and to cherish until we are parted by death" (BCP, 427).

Proclaiming a Mystery

The sermon will fail in its attempt to *explain* what love is about, but perhaps the preacher can describe love well enough for the congregation, including the bride and groom, to identify what the sermon is attempting to proclaim. The words on a pop poster slogan read, "I love you more than yesterday, but not as much as tomorrow." The poster lacks poetry, but it points toward the mystery of the marriage relationship. No couple at their wedding will know what deep partnership is possible between them, but perhaps they can be prepared with hope to expect this wonderful gift as part of Christ's promise in John. A wife nearing her fiftieth anniversary said of her husband, "I know what he is thinking, and I know what he will say before he says it." This is not a complaint about the longevity of their relationship; they are not bored with each other. These words indicate a fulfillment of the promised mystery of two becoming one flesh, of the surprising gift of *agape* growing beyond their expectation. Such rich gifts are only in the making at the time of the marriage, but they can be foretold; and the newly wed can be helped to endure the difficult moments so that the promise may be fulfilled.

Notes:

1. Ian Bunting, *Preaching at Weddings* (Bramcote, Notts, England: Grove Books, 1980), p. 4.

2. Charles P. Price and Louis Weil, *Liturgy for Living* (New York: Seabury, 1979), p. 250.

3. *Ibid.,* p. 253.

4. Edward Schillebeeckx, O.P., *Marriage: Secular Reality and Saving Mystery* (London: Sheed and Ward, 1985), vol. 1, p. 10.

5. Owen C. Thomas, *Introduction to Theology* [revised edition] (Wilton, CT: Morehouse-Barlow Co., Inc., 1983), p. 257.

6. Schillebeeckx, *op. cit.,* p. 18.

7. Rosemary Haughton, *The Theology of Marriage* (Notre Dame, IN: Fides Publishers, Inc., 1971), p. 22.

Preaching at Funerals

Edward Stone Gleason

THE WET MARCH AFTERNOON WAS GRAY, and the foghorn sounded in the harbor every sixty seconds. Four of us were reading silently in front of the fire when we were startled by the telephone. Jim got up and went to the front hall. "It's for you, Ted. Your father. Why not take it upstairs?" He gave no reason for suggesting privacy. I ran up the stairs. Thirty-five years later I can still remember the faded and worn blue stair carpet.

The telephone was between twin beds. I sat down on one and picked up the receiver: "Hello." "Hello," he said. "I have some very bad news. Mother drowned this afternoon. She was swimming alone."

I didn't know what to say. "There must be some mistake."

"No, there's no mistake. The coroner just left. I'll be taking the train up tonight. Meet me at Back Bay, tomorrow evening, 6:24."

What Can Be Said?

I still don't know what to say. There was nothing to say. Nothing. And nothing *was* said. Looking back now on the days that followed my mother's sudden and unexpected death, I remember only the silence. No memorable words were spoken. Yet how much there was that could have been said and should have been said. What might have been proclaimed? What would you have preached at my mother's funeral?

Some might have stood up and said that anyone, anyone at all, who has a mother or a father or a sister or a brother or a wife or a husband or a friend or a child will sooner or later know death. Death happens, that person could have said, and when it does, you will not be ready. No one ever is. Every single one of us knows that death is inevitable, but still we spend most of our life hoping, pretending, even praying, that it will not happen. Not to us, anyway. We block it out and turn away, and then it happens. So it is that the sermon preached at a funeral is first and foremost an opportunity to present clearly and forcefully the reality that is death.

Christ's Love Is Stronger than Death

Several years later, considerably after the deaths of both my mother and father, and after I had become better acquainted with grief and more familiar with sorrow, we came to know a luminous older couple, well married, close to eighty. He was helpless without her. Regardless of his prominence as a scholar, eloquent speaker, and much published author, it was she who made her husband and their marriage work, a marriage that had never been easy, given his bent for self-indulgence. Crippled in both legs and unable to move without help, she made everything flow around her with grace, wherever she was, for she was one of those people who could bring others out of themselves, enabling them to meet each other. Her remarks and insight surpassed those of others, redefining what it meant to be crippled in a facile world.

The most extraordinary thing about her was the way she died. In the final stages of her illness she ordered a hospital bed to be set up in the living room, and the entire afternoon before she died, although in tremendous pain, she received her friends and family. Even at the end, she was making introductions, smoothing the way, putting people at ease. "Grace is new to town. I want you to meet her," she would say. And then, "Elizabeth, you were very kind to bring me that book . . . I'm so glad to see you . . ." As always, immediately before her death, she was at the threshold of something new. That had been true all her life.

All I recall from her funeral was the singing of stanza after stanza of "Ten thousand times ten thousand In sparkling raiment bright, The armies of the ransomed saints Throng up the steps of light," the words of the hymn repeated again and again as we processed from church to graveyard. How appropriate. There is no memory of spoken words, no sermon. There was none. Was this because every aspect of her life was so luminous in the light of Christ that no further proclamation was required? Such was indeed the quality of her life, but here was the opportunity to point out to all who had ears to hear the clear presence of Jesus Christ in the life of one of his own precious saints, one who had dwelled in our very midst. Thanks to the witness of she who had died, those who gathered to mourn her could be assured of the continued presence of the love of Christ in our midst right now, even in the face of death.

Good News in the Face of Death

From all the years of death and burial that have followed, one further story:

He was not an old friend, but we had become congenial colleagues through two years of close association. Work had brought us together and had involved pleasant occasions in each other's houses and many meetings that had included only two or three other people.

The news of his cancer was a shock. Jim was forty-four. The prognosis was good, treatment assured to be successful. Only, the doctors were wrong; and in a few months, death was very near.

Jim was much himself, sitting up in his hospital bed, looking out at the river, when I visited him for the last time. We talked of his youngest child, a son, and of the young woman Jim hoped his son would marry.

"Free advice," Jim had said that day, smiling, but deadly serious.

"Your children are still small. We've been lucky. Our two daughters are married to splendid men. Jane and I love them dearly. They might as well be our own. But I'll tell you. When your child first comes home with that 'best' friend, never tip your hand. You may think the guy is a turkey. But smile, be cordial. Even if you think he's the greatest, don't tell. Remain reserved. Betray no preference. My final wish before I die is that our boy will marry that wonderful girl. They've been together for two years. You've met her. She's perfect. We love her. But we've never let on."

Jim and I laughed, I thanked him, and we prayed. There is no memory of the words we prayed.

Three weeks later, walking up the steps of the small stone church to attend Jim's funeral, I realized that directly in front of us walked his son, hand in hand with *the* young woman. There was no doubt, none, that they would be married. We sat right behind them, just beneath the pulpit. The sermon was outstanding, the best I had heard at a funeral. As we left the church, I congratulated the rector and later wrote him a letter of thanks, asking for a copy of the homily.

He wrote back and said that he had great difficulty preaching at funerals, and that I could find the sermon he had preached that day in such-and-such a book. I did. It read as if written to be preached only at Jim's funeral, powerful and personal, but taken from a book that offered general words to be spoken at the time of death.

Initially puzzled, I gradually realized this obvious fact: the homily preached at a funeral, as at every service of corporate worship, has but *one* primary purpose—to preach the Gospel of Jesus Christ. The homily preached at Jim's funeral proclaimed the Gospel, and in doing so, reached out and included each person present.

Why Preach at Funerals?

The Christian Gospel is rooted in incarnation. Christ's presence is made known through other persons, especially persons who are our friends. Friends are those whom we know and who know us well; their death causes great pain. But just as the Gospel is made known to us through these particular persons, so their death brings the opportunity to celebrate the life and death and the universal power of the Gospel. The particularity of each individual is greatly intensified in and by the Gospel of Jesus Christ.

A funeral is the corporate celebration of the presence of the love, death, and resurrection of Jesus Christ made personal and real in the painful event of the death of a dear friend. The rubric in the Book of Common Prayer that pertains to the sermon on this occasion simply states: "A homily may be preached" (p. 480) or "Here there may be a homily" (p. 495) or "A homily may follow the Readings" (p. 506). If, however, the preacher is motivated by good theology, pastoral concern, and evangelical opportunity, the Burial of the Dead requires a homily.

Death Demands that the Gospel Be Preached and the Gospel Heard

Death is the last great mystery, the event towards which all of life moves, the event we wish to avoid, the event we shall never finally understand. The presence and power of death, however, are proclaimed in the central symbol of the Church: the cross. The Gospel begins with death. Before new life: death. The first task of those who preach at a funeral is to proclaim death, require each person present to lay hold on the real presence and importance of death made so very concrete and immediate in the loss of the person who has just died. The acknowledgement of death opens the door to the possibility of new life; without it, there will be no new life.

In Arthur Miller's autobiographical play, *After the Fall*, the third wife, Holga, describes the dream that haunted her during her years in the Nazi concentration camp. She says of that dream, "The same dream returned each night until I dared not go to sleep and grew quite ill. I dreamed I had a child, and even in the dream I saw it was my life, and it was an idiot, and I ran away. But it always crept onto my lap again, clutched at my clothes. Until I thought, if I could kiss it, whatever in it was my own, perhaps I could sleep. And I bent to its broken face, and it was horrible . . . and I kissed it. I think one must finally take one's own life in one's arms."

No matter how repugnant death may seem, a funeral offers an

opportunity to embrace and proclaim the truth that death opens to us the possibility of new life. If there is to be new life, there must be death. The preacher at a funeral needs to be reminded, and to remind others, that transformation to new life begins *only* through the realization and naming of death, which is ever present and comes in many guises. Because death is our constant companion, the Christian understanding that only through death is the door to new life opened can be revealed to us through several different circumstances and in many forms.

Anticipations of Death

Death is encountered on many a significant occasion before the actual moment when we stop breathing. Consider my friend, Sam, who for almost a decade had operated a successful counseling center in a mid-sized southeastern industrial city. His clients were the major corporate employers who had brought growth and progress to the area. The counseling center offered a full range of services, but the majority of the individuals seeking help struggled with a drinking problem. The center's contract with each employer enabled employees to seek help under a cloak of guaranteed anonymity. The problems and progress of each person were totally private, and it was well known that records were for the eyes of the counseling staff only.

Sam was shocked, therefore, when the Executive Vice President of the largest firm under contract made an appointment and demanded to see all the records for his employees. Sam told the Vice President politely but firmly that this was impossible. The records were completely confidential. The Vice President became irate, red of face, his voice louder and harsher, as he repeatedly insisted that the records for his employees be delivered to him immediately. Sam continued to refuse.

Finally, the Vice President stood up and moved toward the door. As his hand reached out for the knob, he turned and paused. "Very well. Since you insist, tomorrow our legal department will be in touch to terminate our contract with you forthwith. How many of our employees do you suppose availed themselves of your services this year, more than a hundred?" Sam again reminded him that this was confidential information. "No matter. You won't be seeing them anymore unless you let me see their files right now, and I mean *right now*."

"Dick, how many times to I have to tell you? It can't be done. It just can't be done. The work my firm undertakes with your employees is completely confidential. Cancel the contract if you like, but you'll never see those records. Never."

The Vice President turned from the door and walked back to where he had been sitting. "Okay," he said, "if that's the way it is, then I guess it's safe to tell you why I came. I have a drinking problem, and I need your help."

Beyond Death and Eulogy

Important as it is to name death when preaching at a funeral, if this were all the preacher did, Christians would of all people be most miserable. Thanks be to God that we preach not ourselves but Jesus Christ as Lord, and Him present in our midst through the life and death and continued presence of the person who has died.

Preaching at a funeral is not a eulogy. A eulogy is a pre-Christian custom that honors a complete life that has ended, and the eulogy is an attempt to prolong that life, to lend it an air of immortality, to voice the hope that death does not exist but is merely a horizon, the limit of our sight. Preaching at a Christian funeral, however, first and foremost proclaims death. Death has happened, really happened, make no mistake. But that is not all. There is more. What may that be?

One window to the "more" is provided through the life of the dear friend whose death we gather to celebrate. The sermon holds up that life and honors it, not as a eulogy of the individual but as a proclamation of the Gospel of Jesus Christ as it is glimpsed through the life of this person who until a few days ago was in our very midst. As we give thanks for the witness of this person who has died, we are assured of the continued presence of the love of Christ.

As if it were yesterday, I remember one of my dearest friends standing in the pulpit, preaching at the Burial of the Dead about the last six months of his dear young friend, new father of three, dead from cancer. His sermon told the story of that death, the joint exploration of priest and parishioner into what the future held, including the planning of the very service now being experienced by those present. As the sermon drew near its conclusion, the preacher stopped. The silence was lengthy. Then he said this:

"Christopher thought about these things: life, death, resurrection. He decided that the promise we have been given in our Lord and Savior Jesus Christ was true. Of course, it might just not be. The whole thing could be a hoax. Christopher made his decision, and now he lives with his choice. Christopher said yes. Now each of you has to make the same decision. Thanks be to God."

The homily at a funeral, as at every service of corporate worship, has but *one* primary purpose: to preach the Gospel of Jesus Christ. Such a homily will reach out and include each person present.

What Will They Hear?

No matter the occasion, or how many times we have faced death before, death is never a friend. Whether death has come suddenly or after long illness, those who gather at a funeral are bereft. She who was alive is dead and in her place there is sorrow and often shame and guilt—and questions, always questions. Why? Why her? Why now? When will my time come? How? Why? Such primal questions exist even in the minds of people in the congregation only indirectly connected with the person who has died. Yet those who come to a funeral may not be in touch with their own deepest questions and might be unwilling to acknowledge them. The sermon provides the occasion to raise and respond to these unvoiced but heartfelt questions.

The family and close friends at this funeral have walked in numb. The ability to feel has been lost. Whether the death that has brought them here was sudden and terrible or anticipated and serene, they are coping with something overwhelming and incomprehensible. No one can truly say what they know or feel. There is obvious pain and detachment. They arrive saying to you, the preacher: "Reach into my numbness and tell me that death is not the end. Tell me there is more. But don't tell me with hollow, saccharin words. Tell me with profound and personal assurance, born of your faith and the revelation that comes through Christ the Lord." No less challenging are the more peripheral mourners, who may simply think of themselves as fulfilling a social obligation and yet find themselves deeply yearning for assurance and hope.

Such a diverse congregation is united in its need to be fed. A loved one, a friend, a neighbor, a colleague, an acquaintance, a friend's relative—above all, another human being like me—has died. Some who are here today believe that this person is now in the embrace of the risen Christ. They should hear that conviction affirmed. There are others here who have no idea of what has happened; they must be told of the new possibilities and how to embrace them. The preacher's unparalleled opportunity in this sermon is to witness to the saving love of God revealed in One who died on Good Friday and was raised in power on Easter Day.

Death and resurrection are not remote, analytical theories invented in an ancient time and culture to remove the fear and pain of death. Death and resurrection are our constant companions. These we name, describe, and celebrate when we stand to preach at a funeral. As death and resurrection have been our experience, time and time again, through all the days of our life, so too we shall know them in the great day that at last will dawn for each of us. Remember this, and remember well, for this is what all would hear as you prepare to preach in the celebration of death.

The God of peace, who brought again from the dead our Lord Jesus Christ, the great Shepherd of the sheep, through the blood of the everlasting covenant: Make you perfect in every good work to do his will, working in you that which is well-pleasing in his sight; through Jesus Christ, to whom be glory for ever and ever. Amen.

Preaching and the Ministry of Bishops

Frank T. Griswold III

SOMEONE ONCE OBSERVED that the Greek mind-set approaches a topic by analyzing its parts, while the Hebrew method is to illustrate it by telling a story. In considering how I might offer some encouragement for the episcopal ministry of preaching, I find myself drawn toward narrative rather than analysis, and the story I can offer best is my own experience.

The Influence of the Liturgical Movement

One of the principles of the Liturgical Movement which most deeply impressed me about the time I was ordained to the priesthood was the insistence that the Word proclaimed and preached was an integral part of every eucharistic celebration. References were frequently made to the two tables of the Liturgy: the table of the Word and the table of the Eucharist.

Drawing on St. Augustine, one spoke of the Bread of the Word being broken and shared by means of the homily as a parallel to the breaking and sharing of the eucharistic loaf; and in the ordering of liturgical space, the ambo or lectern/pulpit was to be given prominence equal to that of the altar table. The first part of the eucharistic celebration was styled the Liturgy of the Word, and in many churches and religious houses—particularly in Europe—the Bible or the Gospel Book was set apart after the manner of reserving the Blessed Sacrament in order to underscore the truth that God in Christ is indeed present in Sacred Scripture. The revision of the eucharistic lectionary with its three-year cycle of three readings on Sundays and major Feast Days was a further consequence of this new understanding.

Being very much influenced by the Liturgical Movement, especially as it had been brought to Anglican awareness in the 1930's and '40's by the writings of A.G. Hebert and Gregory Dix, I made an informal vow on the eve of my ordination to the priesthood that whenever I presided at the Eucharist, I would always break the bread of the Word and would never proclaim the Gospel without seeking to root it in the hearts and minds of those who were hearing it. With very few exceptions, I have been faithful to this vow with altogether surprising results.

The Word of Scripture and the Word of Life

First of all, this discipline has taught me the necessity of a kind of deep listening, not simply to the Word in Scripture but to the word at the heart of my own life as well. Too often preaching is approached as a domination and domestication of the Word: armed with commentaries and exegesis, we seek to entrap the Word and make it subservient to our own homiletical needs, or use it as a foil for our own cleverness. While such an approach may work with the Sunday liturgy when preparation time can be set aside during the week, it does not work very well on a daily basis when eucharistic celebrations occur at dawn in partial wakefulness, at midday in the midst of a sea of concerns and preoccupations, or in the fatigue of evening. This predictable rhythm is further complicated by the intrusion of unanticipated events, such as an unsettling telephone conversation that has left me disturbed and upset as I rush into the sacristy at the last minute. Perhaps a mood of irritation has descended upon me, or I may be caught up in self-pity or in consideration of my response. At such moments, I don't particularly want to be presiding at the Eucharist: in fact, the liturgy seems to be a singularly unwelcome interruption in my present state. On top of it all, I may have only glanced at the readings in a cursory way or perhaps have done nothing beyond making sure that the ribbon marker is at the right page. Yet my original vow always to break the Word reminds me that I am called, even in such a mood, to submit to the Word and allow it to accost me in the readings at hand so that I may speak a word to others.

As I begin the liturgy, I may feel very poor and unprepared, and perhaps such poverty of spirit permits the Word to touch a deep place within me without my even being aware of it. When the moment comes for the homily, I reach for something within the Scripture which takes me by surprise as it becomes utterance. I hear what I am saying, not only as a word to those present but also as a word to me. Suddenly, I realize that it is a word to me right now in my current state: that it is both born out of and addressed to what is going on within me and the circumstances surrounding me. My surprise and wonderment at such a moment catch me off guard; and so it is that a glimmer of recognition or the nod of a head from the man on the right or the woman on the left encourages and draws out of me a word of life which is for me as well as them. In such a moment the Word, one might say, genuinely becomes incarnate; in such a moment, Christ is truly present.

No less remarkable are those instances in which a particular person—perhaps a recent widow who comes every evening in order to be with others at a point in the day when her loneliness is most acutely felt—pulls a word out of me in response to her own need, a word of hope and trust and endurance which I may need to hear as well, though for quite different reasons. It is indeed a graced and terrible moment to find that one's own needs are so profoundly connected to the faithful declaration of the Word for the gathered community. Such experiences have convinced me that "The word of God is living and active, sharper than any two-edged sword, piercing until it divides soul from spirit, joints from marrow; it is able to judge the thoughts and intentions of the heart" (Hebrews 4:12).

If we allow the Word to pierce us in our poverty—that is, in the actuality and inauspiciousness of this present moment as colored by our mood or preoccupation, it will become for us and for others a word of life in ways beyond our understanding. In this regard, we need to hear and heed the words of Moses to the children of Israel: "The word is very near to you; it is in your mouth and in your heart *ready to be kept*" (Deuteronomy 30:14).[1]

I am not saying for a moment that we should discount critical study of the biblical texts, but sometimes we strain after lofty insights and displays of intellect more undertaken to confirm our sense of competency than to render the Word alive and active in the lives of our hearers. Unless the Word is alive and active in us, there is little chance that it will become life-giving for others, no matter how clever our preachments.

The Life-giving Word

It is also important to acknowledge over and over again that the true minister of the Word, the one who renders it alive and active, is not me but the risen Christ. I remember vividly the release I felt some years ago as I read the account of the disciples who had not recognized Christ on the road to Emmaus, but as they later reflected on the event said to each other, "Were not our hearts burning within us while he was talking to us on the road, *and while he was opening the scriptures to us?*" (Luke 24:32). What suddenly struck me was that the burden of opening the scriptures was not mine but was part of the enduring ministry of the Risen and Living One. This insight gave me a deeper understanding of the resurrection and led me to realize that the charge to proclaim the resurrection does not simply mean to declare a past or future event but to speak out of the experience of resurrection brought about in us by Christ through the opening of the scriptures.

Being aware of such potential for resurrection underscores once again why hearing the Word involves not only listening to the scriptural texts, but also to the word which is alive and active in the turnings of our lives—including our hopes and fears—and in the very specific moments when the words of scripture address us. To be in a place of joy allows me to hear the Word one way, and to be burdened with anxiety disposes me to hear in the very same passage a quite different word. In each case, the idiom of my own life and the scriptural declaration come together and become, as it were, a living and immediate Word which may take the form of a word of illumination or healing or forgiveness or encouragement or purification, depending on what is going on in and around me. But in every case, this living and immediate Word reveals the activity of the risen Christ drawing me out of death into life in all its fullness: into that enlargement of reality we inadequately call resurrection.

The minister of this transformation is the Holy Spirit, for the Spirit draws from what is Christ's: "He will take what is mine and declare it to you" (John 16:15). This drawing and showing is not a matter of some kind of theological abstraction, but rather it involves an appropriation of one's own life and all it contains from the perspective of the mind of Christ. In a very real sense our baptism by water and the Spirit into Christ's death and resurrection allows us to view our own experience, our own history, our own struggles as Christ sees them through the medium of the scriptural word.

The Bishop as Preacher

When I was ordained a bishop, I was very mindful of that portion of the liturgy which asks, "Will you boldly proclaim and interpret the Gospel of Christ, enlightening the minds and stirring up the conscience of your people?" (BCP, p. 518). While such boldness is not limited to the ministry of preaching, the question certainly brought into sharp relief the integral role of proclamation in the exercise of *episcope* or oversight.

Being determined not to become a "one sermon" bishop who had an annual sermon which was indiscriminately preached regardless of the Scripture appointed for the day, I decided to ground myself on each occasion in the provisions of the lectionary. Carefully prepared with notes and all the rest, I started out on my visitations to the congregations of the diocese I serve. What I had not anticipated was the diversity of those 144 congregations and the wide variety of their liturgical temperaments, including (but not limited to) how they received the Word proclaimed and preached.

In my anxiety about being effective as a preacher, I had in some ways over-prepared and as a consequence lacked sufficient flexibility to adjust to the incarnate reality of the particular congregation I was visiting. The difficulty was further compounded by the fact that week after week I found myself standing before assemblies of virtual strangers. The kind of rapport I had known with my congregation as a parish priest—a rapport which was the fruit of months and years of pastoral relationship and liturgical celebration—was now largely nonexistent. As bishop I was no longer familiar friend and pastor but was cast in the role of an infrequent visitor who wore an odd pointed hat. In many places notions of hierarchy epitomized in the episcopal person reinforced and widened a sense that there was a great gulf fixed between the pulpit and the pews.

In moving from place to place I learned a great deal about each congregation's expectations of the preacher. If people were eager-eyed and expectant, I could assume that they were accustomed to being edified and fed from the riches of God's Word and that the local clergy took seriously their call to proclaim the Good News. If, on the other hand, a pall of disinterest descended upon the assembly, I could assume that preaching in that congregation was a largely lifeless affair. Especially in these situations, my task then became one of breaking through such indifference and laying claim to the worshipping community's consciousness in the name of Christ.

Occasionally random circumstances tangential to the act of preaching have helped to this end. I remember once having launched into a sermon in a rather affluent suburban congregation only to discover that my hearers were regarding me from behind an invisible shield of total impermeability. I raised my voice and became more passionate, but to no avail. Inadvertently, my right hand, sporting a very large amethyst ring which had belonged to two former bishops of the diocese, struck the side of the pulpit, producing a large crack over the very sensitive public address system. People jumped in their pews, and I—with some irritation at my ineptitude—waved my ringed hand toward the congregation and exclaimed, "A friend of mine upon seeing this ring remarked, 'No decent woman would wear a stone like that before five o'clock in the afternoon.' " Gasps ensued, followed by nervous giggles, which soon relaxed into laughter. Then I began again and found the former gulf was no longer there.

That unplanned moment taught me that episcopal preachers must in some way become accessible as persons in order for the congregations to whom they are preaching to receive the Word and keep it. Clearly one cannot rap one's episcopal ring against the side of every pulpit or resort to a succession of gimmicks without undermining one's integrity. The most effective and honest way to become accessible to a congregation is simply to preach out of one's lived faith. When recalling that the Examination of the ordination rite speaks of a bishop as "called to be one with the apostles in proclaiming Christ's resurrection and interpreting the Gospel" (BCP, p. 517), it is important to keep in mind that the apostles were not first of all ecclesiastical functionaries, but persons who had lived in intimacy with Jesus and had experienced personally and collectively Christ's dying and rising as the core reality of their lives.

Christ's Life and Ours

How has the Paschal mystery touched the deep places of my own life? How is it touching them now? Where have dying and rising occurred in me, and altered my perceptions, and called me to an enlargement of consciousness? How is this Scripture lesson Good News for me? What are some of the obstructions and areas of resistance in me and the patterns of my life which undermine my "doing the truth" in responsible to the Word?

These are some of the questions which move within me as I face not only the task of preaching but the other dimensions and demands of life and episcopal ministry as well. Indeed, what becomes clearer and clearer is that preaching and praying and living are profoundly one. All these have to do with a growing availability to God's Word in Scripture and in our own lives—each word illuminating the other—as well as the courage to accept Christ's challenge to "hear the Word of God and keep it" (Luke 11:27).

Note:

1. Most quotations of Scripture in this essay follow the New Revised Standard Version. There are two exceptions: the italicized section at the end of this quotation and the passage from Luke at the very end, both of which follow the New English Bible.

Preaching and the Potential of Liturgical Space

William Seth Adams

ANYONE WHO HAS EVER read a copy of a sermon previously heard knows that the typescript does not recreate the original experience of it. The power and vitality of the sermon are difficult to reconstitute from the printed page, even for the most imaginative reader. Although it certainly consists of words that can be written down, a sermon delivered in a liturgical context is conveyed or accomplished by breath, voice, gesture, posture, glance, intonation, location. All these elements contribute to the preaching event and are lost from the sermon "copy," save in the imagination. Even the audio recordings many parishes make as part of their ministry to hospitalized or homebound members fail to capture more than the sound; they cannot impart the other aspects that combine to produce the experience of actually being present.

Patricia Wilson-Kastner provides a helpful approach to this phenomenon. In her fine insightful book *Imagery for Preaching*, she writes, "Rooted in the liturgy, preaching shares in [the eucharistic liturgy's] visible, tangible, sensory character."[1] Visible, tangible, sensory. Indeed! Preaching is by its very nature an embodied act, a physical part of our common ritual life. The written text is no more fully descriptive of the sermon than the formulas in the Prayer Book are exhaustive of the Sunday morning liturgy. Though we have tried over the years to separate rite and ceremony, sermon and delivery, surely we know that they are integral to each other.

Furthermore, because it is something physical and embodied, preaching "takes place." That is, preaching has about it not only physicality but also spatiality.[2] In considering these combined factors, we shall explore the physical and spatial dimensions of Christian proclamation, taking the gathered eucharistic community as the normative setting. In this exploration, it is our intent to consider how the liturgical environment can be used to enhance preaching.

A Place for Preaching

As Marion Hatchett has reminded us, the design of the liturgical space in our day is, and must be, informed by the architectural expectations of the liturgy itself.[3] The fundamental requirement imposed on the design of such a space has two facets. First, consideration must be given to the location of the three liturgical centers in association with which the liturgical action is accomplished. These three centers—or better, "places"—are distinguished by their own particular ritual object: the font marks the place for initiation, the altar/table indicates the place for "Holy Communion," and the ambo (pulpit, lectern) identifies the place for "the Word of God."[4]

A second facet of the design process is determining the shape of the room, identifying the spatial environment for the configuration of the several centers and other constituent elements so that seeing and hearing are available to all. Obviously the location of the liturgical centers should influence the shape of the room, rather than the other way around. In addition, the ecclesiology of the Prayer Book being what it is, the shape of the liturgical room ought to make possible some measure of face-to-face access for the congregation. Though actually sitting around a table is not critically important to the point, Rudolf Arnheim is surely right in saying, "When people face one another across a table, they testify to their convivial status, that is, to their 'living together' for the occasion. The audience in the usual theater or lecture hall possesses a mere parallelism of purpose and target, which is quite different from doing things *with* other people."[5]

Perhaps, by now it is not necessary to say more about the appropriateness of "gatheredness" in the design of our liturgical rooms. Nor perhaps is it any longer necessary to argue the appropriateness of reading the Bible and preaching the sermon from the same place. It seems increasingly common in new churches—and in the remodeling of existing ones—for the ambo to replace the older combination of lectern and pulpit. In such a room, the single ambo would suggest that the reading and preaching done in that place are constituent elements of the same proclamation. The visual or spatial integrity and unity of the proclamation, of course, would depend on the way in which the proclamation space was actually used.

At issue here is a sense of place, and the potential conflict between the spatial signals of "emplacement" and the physical or embodied evidence. It is not uncommon in the Episcopal Church to experience the various aspects of proclamation—readings, psalmody, and preaching—occurring at different locations throughout the room. The ambo, as a single place of proclamation, would gather all these up, *if* the ambo were so used. Sadly, in many congregations, wherever the reading and psalmody may occur, the preaching is done in a place-less fashion. This "no-place" is often the altar rail gate, the chancel step, or the head of the central aisle. Preaching from "no-place" seems to encourage physical wandering, an aimlessness mirrored far too often in the sermon itself. Preaching from "no-place" gives the homily an occasional, transient character which hardly dignifies the Word of God.

Those who engage in this kind of preaching in the ordered liturgy of the church are apparently seeking not only a more conversational style but also more access to and intimacy with the congregation. To the extent that such qualities are desirable for proclamation, having to seek them in "no-place" is a clear judgment on the design of the room itself, a testimony to the failure of the design to serve the liturgy.

This practice raises then the matter of the location of the ambo. What the Prayer Book holds up for the church in the Holy Eucharist is the clear conviction and expectation that the eucharistic rite is composed of two constituent parts, the Word of God and Holy Communion, and that these two parts associated with their respective ritual objects, are *of equal value and power in the rite.* From this premise we can argue that the ritual objects ought to be placed in the room in such a fashion as to show forth this mutuality and interrelationship.

Unfortunately, what the Prayer Book sets out in the Holy Eucharist has yet to find consistent spatial expression in the Episcopal Church. Instead of mutuality and reciprocity between the objects and what they signal, we continue to build rooms in which one object dominates the other: i.e., the altar/table is typically central and the ambo is typically not. This circumstance is no doubt due in great measure to the residual dominance of a particular historical and architectural tradition aided by teachings growing out of the eucharistic reawakening of which the Prayer Book itself is a part. To speak of the church as being eucharistically centered often gets translated into buildings which are altar-centered. In contrast to this single dominant feature, what the Prayer Book actually teaches, as we have suggested already, is that a eucharistically centered room would have as its focus a pair of objects, ambo and altar/table, which *together* signal the unity of the Word and Holy Communion, at least for those with "eyes to see."

What we are proposing is that the ambo and the altar/table be placed in the room in a mutually central place, neither being dominant over the other, neither in fact being on the central axis of the room. What would be central would be the pair, their mutuality and their balance being clearly set forth. This would mean they would share a common elevation and a common platform. Since they would have different volumes, they would need to be placed and proportioned appropriately in order to achieve visual balance. In practice, this would probably mean that one might well be forward of the other, each on its own side of the

William Seth Adams

central axis. Symmetry, per se, is not the issue; balance is.

Such a "place" of corresponding dignity would be the normative center for proclamation—readings, psalmody, preaching. Such a place would be the location from which the church would rightly and habitually expect to hear the Word of God.

The Embodiment of the Word

Having considered how the proclamation of the Word of God requires a sense of place capable of showing forth the intimate relation between such proclamation and the enactment of visible words in the church's sacraments, we need now to consider the matter from a slightly different direction. From *emplacement* we move to *embodiment.*

Once again, the work of Patricia Wilson-Kastner provides us with a starting place. Dr. Wilson-Kastner writes very ably about the necessity of imagery for powerful preaching:

> Of particular importance to preachers is the growing recognition that verbal, abstract expression is the province of a few, whereas the visual, sensory and imagery-filled discourse is accessible to virtually everyone. This fact does not mean that preaching is only about the physical world or is confined to what we say and hear. But effective preaching is rooted and focused in the physical and sensory.[6]

Later she adds,

> [T]he imagery in a sermon encompasses the verbal descriptions and evocations of the visual, tactile, auditory and all other dimensions of the physical world.[7]

Surely, she is right. Effective, persuasive preaching requires the union of rational and sensory-affective dimensions of human knowing. Physicality is constitutive of human being. In our preaching, the more seriously we take our embodiment, the more effective will be our proclamation. As one ponders this insight and is persuaded of its truth, the more one is drawn, ineluctably, into reflections on the physical act of preaching itself.

One of the joys of our liturgical tradition and especially our current liturgical texts is their remarkable combination of stability and variation. Obviously, it is the nature of the liturgy to be repetitive, creating a stability into which the community enters when it gathers, being formed and reformed as the Body of Christ. For many this stability, predictability, and familiarity provide a most powerful place of access to God and God's graciousness. In the presumed "safety" of this stability, we allow ourselves to be vulnerable to the Holy One. The formative influence of the liturgy is keenly experienced through the stability of the liturgy.

Yet, the "ordinary" part of the liturgy is enriched and enlivened by things "proper" to the day or season. In this fashion the vitality of God's companionship with us is recounted in various ways, the church year being the principal instrument directing our attention. The cadence of the church year is sufficiently methodical and its impact sufficiently subtle that this variety is welcome and nourishing, rather than disruptive and threatening.[8]

This combination of variety and stability is common to our liturgical life. Together these two features protect us on the one hand from becoming static or on the other of being rootless. Working in concert they engage our humanity more fully and provide us a richer experience of the presence and intention of God.

The inevitable impact of the calendar on preaching is obvious and very important. As mediated through the lectionary, the "stuff" of the calendar becomes the "stuff" of the church's proclamation. It is the calendar—especially as it is expressed in the lectionary—that provides focus, support, and direction for the proclamation. The lectionary makes our preaching "timely," and therefore rich and varied.[9]

Now if we add to this notion of timeliness an increased attention to the sensory-affective dimension of human being and knowing, we come to some interesting possibilities, even adventurous suggestions about the proclamation. All these suggestions grow out of the conviction that the physicality of preaching can be intensified in a timely way, and that doing so will add to the vitality of the homiletical life of the church.

William Seth Adams

Imagining Some Possibilities

Imagine for the moment that the parish liturgy committee was about the work of planning the services for a particular day or season. In such a setting it would be appropriate and hardly surprising that questions arise about themes and emphases, and about how these themes might be carried out or expressed liturgically. More surprising, however, would be the questions we would urge upon this group. In addition to questions about the way the liturgy should carry the theme, we might ask: How shall we preach? That is, given that the proclamation is the church's proclamation, what shall we say on this day or season and how shall we say it? These are likely to be new questions for both preacher and liturgy committee, but in our current exploration they are appropriate questions. How shall we "say" our preaching?

Once given permission to wonder about this, or being persuaded that imagining an answer to this question has integrity, it is difficult to know what sort of faithful answer might be forthcoming. It might only be limited by the amount of the energy of God's Spirit we were willing to invest in the enterprise!

Some examples. During seasons in which movement toward a destination is characteristic of and integral to the spirituality of things, the preaching might be done so as to intensify that sense of movement. Preaching from "stations," as it were, set in a sequence toward some particular destination could add genuine power to the keeping of the season. The destination certainly need not be the altar. If, for instance, in a parish preparing a group of catechumens for baptism at the Easter Vigil, preparation in which the congregation had an obvious investment and involvement, then the stational sermons might "progress" toward the font. This would mark the journey of all the baptized, soon to be replicated by the catechumens. This kind of preaching would be largely a verbal undertaking enlivened by intentional progressive movement.

Another set of possibilities would involve the reduction of spoken language in favor of other "language" forms. In this approach, the spoken words would be at most the companion or servant of some other "language." Among the potential examples, the first and most dramatic possibility would be the use of mime as a vehicle for proclamation. In this case, no spoken words would occur at all, save *perhaps* the reading of the text. If the pantomime were both the "reading" and the "sermon," then silence (or music) would be all that was heard. This physical visualization would carry to fullest expression the line of reasoning we have appropriated from Patricia Wilson-Kastner's remarks quoted earlier. The "sermon" would be *wholly* "visual, sensory and imagery filled."[10]

A second kind of less-verbal art form for preaching would be exemplified by the combination of art or music and words. Careful collaboration between speaker/preacher and visual artist or musician can yield wonderful results. The contrast between abstract verbal expressions and music, between the externality of even powerful verbal imagery and the engulfing character of music could certainly be integrated in rewarding ways. Any sermon dealing with matters of harmony and discord might well be served by a "score" to accompany the "libretto" provided by the reading. Even a story like that of the Prodigal could be faithfully scripted and scored so as to edify the congregation. What a challenge it would be to the musician to score a part for the older brother, surely the "everyman/everywoman" of the parable!

In a similar way, the careful collaboration of a preacher and visual artist can yield equally powerful results. Whether the artist works toward something representational or abstract, whether the artist's work is created "on the spot" or beforehand, line and color can—as surely as music—convey the sinews and texture of proclamation. In my own experience this approach has been used in a strong and captivating way, by the artist and preacher doing the textual exegesis and hermeneutical preparation together until each and both had an "aha!" The "aha" then became the matter for proclamation in the liturgy. The artist and preacher made their mutual proclamation by working simultaneously so that the words and the art piece were concluded at the same time, making the same point.

Handled effectively, either music or visual art can serve as a useful form of proclamation for children, who are, one hopes, more and more a part of the eucharistic community. The same observation holds true for mime and for any combination of physical action and words.

Another personal experience, this time from "preaching" on Luke 13:20, the parable in which the reign of God is said to be "like leaven." The preacher accomplished the sermon by doing very little speaking but by investing considerable energy in mixing bread dough. The mixing was done in the "crossing" of the building. What little was said came from the perspective of a "baker" who struggled with the dough and spoke of the uncontrollable nature of yeast: "there is in this dough of mine a trickster, a mysterious living power set loose . . . which will change what I plan, what I imagine. It is beyond my control. It works its own work, in spite of me." Such is leaven and the Reign of God. Most of what occurred in the "sermon" was visual and physical, and one hopes also edifying. (The bread was subsequently baked and eaten.)

To these examples could certainly be added the often illuminating effects of drama. As exposition and elaboration of a text, drama can be a good preacher and evangelist. The same is true of liturgical dance. Yet another option might be variations of the dialogue sermon in which several speakers are involved, perhaps located at various points in the room. This might be an effective way to stage a debate between Jesus and his detractors or to narrate sections of Job. Certainly this list and these examples could be expanded greatly. But neither these nor others should be considered unless the "staging" is done with great care, the same care as the rest of the liturgy. As a minimal consideration for any of these methods to be employed, the people must tolerate it, the building must tolerate it, and certainly the "preacher" must tolerate it. Only all these factors working in concert will prove fertile ground for proclamation.

Balancing the "Ordinary" and the "Proper"

In conclusion, we need to gather up the concern of the first part of this essay and the concern of the second. Initially we advocated the spatial union of the aspects of proclamation—reading, psalmody, preaching—into a single "place." This place, the ambo, was offered as the *normative* location for proclamation, clearly preferable to visual fragmentation of the readings and to preaching from "no-place." In the second section, we have suggested that preaching take a more physical form and take on a spatial expression which makes more expansive use of the liturgical space.

In order to reconcile these apparently contradictory ideas, we need to return to the interplay of "ordinary" and "proper," an interplay focused by the issue of timeliness. Simply put, if the norm is well fixed, then timely variations from it have their "place" and can be profoundly effective and powerful. This would mean in practice that the ambo would be the "ordinary" place, and an oration the "ordinary" style. Such would be the typical, predictable, and expected norm. However, variations in a timely, "proper" fashion could occur. Without the solid support and foundation of the norm, timeliness cannot happen; unstabilized innovation yields chaos, by which the community of the faithful is not edified nor is God glorified. What we propose then is "seasoning" the norm, bringing to that norm a "proper" vitality. This balance of stability and variety in the proclamation of the Gospel, experienced in a disciplined way over time, would surely enliven the Word as it becomes flesh again in the lives of God's people.

Notes:

1. (Minneapolis: Fortress Press, 1989), p. 14.

2. Regarding the matter of "place," the following might be useful: Kent C. Bloomer and Charles W. Moore, *Body, Memory, and Architecture* (New Haven: Yale University Press, 1977); Christian Norbert-Schulz, *The Concept of Dwelling* (New York: Rizzoli, 1985); and Jonathan Z. Smith, *To Take Place* (Chicago: U. of Chicago Press, 1987).

3. "The Architectural Implications of the Book of Common Prayer" [Occasional Paper Number Seven (March 1985)] in *The Occasional Papers of the Standing Liturgical Commission: Collection Number One* (New York: Church Hymnal Corporation, 1987), pp. 57–66.

4. In this essay, only two of these three centers will be considered. For treatment of the third, the font, see my article, "De-coding the Obvious: Reflections on Baptismal Ministry in the Episcopal Church," *Worship*, 66:4 (July 1992), 327–338, to be reprinted in a supplemented form in a forthcoming set of Occasional Papers to be published by the Standing Liturgical Commission.

5. *The Dynamics of Architectural Form* (Berkeley: U. of California Press, 1977), p. 269.

6. *Imagery for Preaching*, p. 13.

7. *Ibid.*, p. 48.

8. On the impact of the church year, see Christopher Kiesling, "The Formative Influence of Liturgy," *Studies in Formative Spirituality*, 3:3 (November 1982), 377–385.

9. Some of what follows is dependent on flexible or variable liturgical space. On this subject see my article, "An Apology for Variable Liturgical Space," *Worship*, 61:3 (May 1987), 231–242.

10. *Imagery for Preaching*, p. 13.

Breaking the Word
for a Broken World

Preaching and Pastoral Care

John H. Snow

ONCE WHEN I WAS ON VACATION, I heard a particularly unfortunate sermon in which the preacher kept referring to what he called "passive-dependent Christians." In some detail he described Christians who, he said, believed that not only God but also the church would take care of them as if they were small children. Such people, the preacher claimed, gave little or nothing to the church and never volunteered to teach church school or carry their share of the every-member canvass, yet still expected the church to provide Christian education for their children, marry and bury them, provide Sunday worship, and visit them when they were sick. Throughout the sermon, the preacher kept repeating the words "passive-dependent" in a voice touched with vague disdain.

Preaching as Admonition

There is a great deal of precedent for this kind of admonishing sermon, and it goes all the way back to St. Paul. It is also a part of the minister's pastoral responsibilities, though most ministers find such sermons a chore. Some simply avoid them in order to avoid sounding like a common scold. Yet if the pastor sees evidence of a fair amount of shared behavior in parish life that is destructive of actual mutuality, the matter should probably be addressed.

St. Paul's way of doing this is worth noting. He could be quite scathing about behavior in the community that did not contribute to the common life, yet behind everything he said was the assumption that such behavior could—indeed would—be changed. Paul might also accuse a congregation of childish behavior, of needing milk rather than the meat of the mature. But he expected mature behavior, for in his practice of ministry Paul had a very robust doctrine of human freedom.[1]

It might be argued today that it is not the job of the parish minister to change people's behavior. Who is this person to lecture a group of adults on how they should behave? Isn't it this patriarchal or matriarchal role that leads to the infantilization of the laity? The answer to this question is simple enough. The priest has been chosen by the congregation to articulate and iterate a traditional consensus about what constitutes moral interaction among Christians.[2]

Preaching That Makes a Difference

The clinical-sounding phrase so often repeated by that vacation-time preacher was doubtless wielded as part of his authority. It bore testimony to his familiarity with counseling theory, or at least some of its jargon. But was it an appropriate use? How and whether counseling theory should be used in preaching cannot be addressed without considering the prior question of the relationship of preaching to pastoral care and parish ministry.

First, when I speak of preaching here, I am not speaking of the delivery of a single memorable sermon but of the cumulative effect of preaching Sunday after Sunday, year after year, to a congregation that is relatively stable, at least within its particular demographic or economic situation. It is this cumulative effect that is ultimately so important, yet preaching is often thought of as the preparation of discrete sermons, each an occasion in itself.

Even when the preacher focuses only on the construction and delivery of individual sermons, a cumulative effect will be present. The preacher's philosophy will, over the years, become manifest to the congregation and may even be adopted by a number of parishioners as a way to make sense out of their existence. Or it may become evident that the preacher has no substantial theology at all, just an overlay of theological clichés to give the odor of sanctity to a simple empirical view of life. This, too, will affect the nature of pastoral care understood as the construction of a world in which people live and move and have their being.

Yet the world constructed is more likely to reflect the underlying empiricism than the pious overlay. There are churches in the United States that are almost entirely pragmatic and instrumental, rationalized down to the last committee. Their public relations efforts are generated by a professional firm. They have an Olympic-sized pool, an indoor running track, a health food bar, a fully computerized office and all the rest. Such churches tend to be fundamentalist in their preaching, even to the point of castigating as Satanic or un-American anything vaguely therapeutic. Interestingly enough this pulpit rhetoric seems not to affect their counseling centers (if they have them) which will often dispense therapeutic insights and solutions.

Such churches may seem irrelevant to Episcopalians, but they demonstrate a conflict in which we also participate. In the Episcopal Church, the sermons preached on Sunday morning are just as likely to be at odds with the parish world that has actually been constructed. From the pulpit come exhortations to love, to be just, to be compassionate, to be inclusive, while the fund-raising methods, the election of the vestry, or the calling of a minister can be as harshly competitive as anything found in the corporate world.

The primary purpose of preaching is to let the Gospel be known, apprehended, and taken as the good news of our salvation through Jesus Christ, the news that love has overcome death and we are ultimately safe. But if we begin to accept this good news as true, then it has consequence for how we live our lives together. Our liberation from bondage to sin and death not only makes us feel good, it also affects our corporate life. This, then, is the function of preaching in pastoral care: edification, building up, the construction of a world.

What Do We Build Up?

I think that the modern church has made a great mistake in interpreting this work of edification too empirically, seeing it in terms of building actual communities within the parish. Through insights borrowed from group dynamics and human potential techniques, we have attempted to build joyous, generous, open, warm, and healthy communities in our parishes. Where we succeeded, we built very exclusive communities for white middle-class college graduates. To have a sense of belonging in such communities was to commit oneself to the values and rules delivered to the parish through the preaching of the minister—who was fresh from this lab or that institute. Those who accepted this model benefited from it in many ways. They did become more sensitive to others, particularly in group interaction. Many discovered their feelings, were able to name them and to be conscious of them for the first time, and so could live with them without being tyrannized by them. Some people learned a kind of self-acceptance that made them less defensive and devious in dealing with their neighbors, and they learned to celebrate this community joyfully.

Where they were successful, such parishes served the personal well-being of parishioners as well as the health of their families. They may even have contributed to the good of the greater society by sending people into it who knew who they were, who were sensitive to others and "felt good" about themselves. However these people did not have any particular ethical orientation, or, indeed, any particular values beyond the therapeutic goals of adaptivity, maturity, and the reduction of conflict—free, smooth functioning with perhaps a little kindness thrown in. They were nice, pleasant, happy people, who seemed to prosper in their love and work, which was no small thing; as Freud said, it is the basic sign of health.

Preaching within this parish model tended to be couched in the language of personal development and growth, all with a pious overlay. It is surprisingly easy to go through the New Testament and find all kinds of scriptural texts that seem to confirm counseling theory about human interaction. Two especially popular passages: "Be angry and sin not" (Ephesians 4:26) meant "Express your negative feelings in order to get rid of them," while "If . . . you suddenly remember your brother has a grievance against you, . . . first go and make peace with your brother" (Matthew 5:24) was a directive about conflict. Don't avoid it. Confront it and work through it.

To lift isolated exhortations from the New Testament and use them outside of any context whatever as a bolster for therapeutic insights is a fundamentalism in search of proof texts. Such preaching, however, confirmed and maintained and rationalized and interpreted the world that was being constructed by adult education curricula, church school teacher training, counseling, and even the committees and task groups of the parish.

Counseling Theory and Social Justice

During the heyday of this model in the early sixties, very little serious attention was given in preaching (or in any other way) to the community beyond the parish, or to social justice on the national scene. Despite some vivid exceptions, insularity was the widespread norm. When the civil rights movement began to make itself felt, it made its first impact through preaching, and the results were unexpected. As Don Browning likes to point out, ordained ministers tended to assume that the "value-free" aspects of counseling theory operated within a context of traditional Christian ethics. These ministers were simply unaware of the extent to which therapeutic culture, as it was expressed in the form of "pop psychology" by the media, had enveloped the moral and ethical values of the parish.

The assumed values of pulpit and pew were further separated by the clarity of the biblical witness on this issue. Seen from a New Testament perspective, racism is a simple ethical problem. It goes against the very heart of the Gospel's revelation of the nature of

God. It is so wrong as to be blasphemous. To many ministers this seemed so obvious that saying so hardly seemed controversial. Yet many Episcopalians were confused by what seemed to them a new turn toward social ethics, and the result was conflict within the parish. Leaving aside the solid block of hardcore racists in the church, who were as opposed to counseling theory as they were to racial equality, the more usual reaction in white suburban churches to preaching for racial justice was likely to be, "Don't bother me with things over which I have no control. I am concerned with being a healthy person, making a difference where I am. Your bringing politics and ideology into the pulpit makes me feel bad about things I can't really change."

The "I didn't do it, I can't change it, don't blame me" attitude was itself tied to certain assumptions of counseling theory. Persons who showed an intense concern for matters beyond the range of their own family, work, and social environment were said to be "having problems"—with relationships in the family, at work, or in their social life. Social activism was regarded by those influenced by the human potential movement as simply a matter of projecting inner conflicts onto society and trying to resolve them there. This kind of thinking led to easy trivialization of social issues, so that the very attitudes which the clergy had themselves encouraged and fostered led some parish ministers to lose their credibility in the pulpit when their parishioners adopted those assumptions.

It must be admitted that in some cases there were grounds for criticism. Preachers would blame and rant at congregations who showed no interest in social justice. Sermons became predictable and boring and in one sense neurotic; they were accomplishing the opposite of what they were intended to do, hardening people to the issue of racial justice and creating a well of hostility towards the preacher. There was even some degree of truth in the criticism that such sermons were projections of personal concerns, since imagination and empathy are inherently distorted somewhat by individual experience. But imagination and empathy are the heart of ethical commitment, and where they are naively and uncritically accepted as sufficient reason for ethical action ("I feel it should be obvious to anyone that what I am doing is right"), then they are hugely untrustworthy as a source of motivation.

Ironically enough, other ministers who were well trained in counseling theory and group process provided a new kind of social activist leadership. They exercised leadership that was committed and assertive, yet sensitive to group process and to the pain and conflict of individuals, including the adversary. These ministers knew about projection; they were aware of the dangers of escaping from one's own real problems by hurling oneself into the movement. They were constantly checking out themselves and one another on their motivations to keep them from fouling up the real purpose of the movement.

Perhaps the most notable preacher and leader of this sort was Martin Luther King, Jr. Sometimes we forget that he got his training at Boston University School of Theology, for years the most counseling-oriented seminary in the United States. The first time I heard King preach was in 1961 to a congregation of students at Williams College. His sermon on that occasion relied heavily on his psychological sophistication, dealing primarily with the question of balance in the inner life and the importance of self-esteem. Race was hardly mentioned, although at that time he was in the middle of leading the Montgomery bus boycott.

But self-esteem was mentioned, and King's stature as a leader resulted from his ability to take this single concept from counseling theory and assimilate it into a biblical theology. And I think it was rightly and appropriate assimilated, because Jesus, in his encounters with the poor and the sick, was intensely aware of their self-regard. Jesus did not tell them how good they were, he simply loved them and they began to want to become good. Think of the disbelief expressed by the Samaritan woman at the well in John 4. She was astonished that Jesus even spoke to her, and how animated, witty, and theologically acute she became as she realized that Jesus, the Messiah, was speaking to her in full knowledge of who she was and how she had lived her life.

Two decades later, American leadership (epitomized by Ronald Reagan) also emphasized the importance of self-esteem, but in an ethical and religious vacuum. Instead of confirming the divine image in people, with its potential for responding to the demands of justice and love, this era confirmed the greedy, violent, selfish, competitive behavior of people, telling them that it was okay, the American way.

Though King and Reagan addressed people to quite different ends, each was effective through understanding that there has been and continues to be a chronic national questioning of self-esteem. Indeed, the issue seems to be an important one in all developed countries, because it is inevitably tied to science and technology and the empirical worldview that goes with them. Where all important issues are set as problems to be solved, and the bottom line can or should always be quantified, it is hard to see the importance of one human being—if only because nothing really important is solved in life and, we are constantly being told, there are far too many human beings on this planet. Where this reductionist, scientific self-definition is endemic in culture, it is not hard to see why we might listen to anyone who even suggested that we were of some value. This need of ours lies at the center of cult dynamics as well.

Self-Esteem and Preaching

All of this has considerable significance for preaching. I once heard one of the more famous preachers in the Episcopal Church say in a lecture on preaching, "When I preach, I always go for a conviction." This is the classic mode of preaching for conversion. One convicts one's listeners in the congregation, defines them as hopeless sinners alienated from God and neighbor, and then presents them with a God who would care for them if only they would let him. (I say "him" advisedly, because for these preachers God is a strict father who has been disobeyed or ignored.)

People still like this kind of preaching, but for curious reasons. They like it first of all because it defines the way they feel about themselves and so confirms their sanity. They learn that they are not the only people who feel this way. Then, since their belief in the God who has saved or will save them from this state is minimal, belief for them is empirical, totally dependent on "the facts." They hear a curious message that it is all right—indeed, simply a part of the human condition—to be the sinners they are. Because they find not only their sinful condition but also their sinful behavior confirmed, they see no need or even possibility for repentance. People enjoy this kind of preaching because, as they interpret it, it makes no real demands on them: there is no need to change. At the same time, it helps to make preachers feel like prophets and strengthens their own self-image as people of integrity.

Finding a Theological Understanding of Self-Regard

This issue of self-regard is absolutely critical to parish ministry today, yet it is also one of the most theologically difficult issues the church faces. Counseling theory sees self-esteem as lying at the heart of all healthy and adaptive behavior towards self and others. To the extent that this theory is derived from Freud, it assumes that self-esteem—feeling comfortable with oneself, having a healthy ego, whatever you want to call it—is based on basic trust, the result of a first year of adequate parenting.[3]

At various times in its history Christianity has looked at the self in different ways. The gospels' primary statement about self is the second dominical commandment, "Thou shalt love thy neighbor as thy self"; yet elsewhere in the New Testament we are urged to die to ourselves, to deny ourselves, to humble ourselves. Self-congratulation is a mark of spiritual pride: the Pharisee, for example, who prayed in the temple before the tax collector is said to pray "with himself." The New Testament also uses "self" as we would use "ego": the prodigal son comes to himself, Peter in Acts comes to himself, Jesus' family say that he is "beside himself." Here the word "self" is defined as the sane and good core of the person, the real, conscious, unique center.[4]

This all gets translated into another internal argument of Christianity: between agape and eros, between faith and works. Where the self is seen as bad, "selfish," greedy, concupiscent, and—above all—'proud,' personal piety is based on agape and faith. One surrenders to the love of God by faith. Works, even pious works of prayer and charity, do not help. If you believe Anselm or even

Karl Barth, there is nothing about the self worth redeeming. The fact of its having been made in the image of God is irrelevant compared to the enormity of Adam's sin. Our salvation is entirely in God's hands. In the extreme Calvinist position even our response to God's love is in God's hands.

Where the emphasis is put on the self's similarity to the image and likeness of God, where the self has intrinsic value simply as a creature of God and sin is not understood as a genetic inheritance from Adam but as a form of captivity to Satan and the kingdom of death, piety can follow at least two ways. In his book *Agape and Eros* (Philadelphia: Westminster Press, 1953), Anders Nygren calls these two ways the erotic and the nomic. Both are self-centered, human centered.

Eros piety evaluates everything on the basis of its helpfulness in leading us to God. Thus, we are loving in order to become closer to God; we pray and follow an ascetic path in order to become closer to God. Everything we touch is used in our spiritual quest to become perfect, or perhaps to become perfectly ourselves in becoming more like God. Nothing is valued for its own sake, or even for Christ's sake, but only for its usefulness to us in our spiritual quest.

The nomic variation on this theme is to make Christianity the new law, which is basically the old law but more rigorous. Anybody can love one's neighbors; love your enemy. Anyone can fast in public, let's see you do it in private. Anyone can keep from committing adultery, but can you keep from thinking about sex at all? Nygren calls this nomic strain the Jewish influence, and the erotic strain, Greek.

True Christianity, he believes, is a religion of agape and is based on dying to the worthless self, submitting wholly to God's grace and letting it fill our whole being. Out of gratitude we let it enable us to love others as God loves us, with a love that has no motive but our gratitude to God. We do not love others because it gets us into heaven or because loving the good, the true, and the beautiful in others provides basic training in loving God. We simply love them, however stupid or ugly they are; we care what happens to them. We want justice for them; we want to keep them from evil and suffering; we want to serve them. We do this cheerfully, out of the knowledge that God loves us not because of ourselves, but in spite of ourselves.

Agape Christianity as it was preached in the fifties really had no place for human goodness.[5] It was dead set against preaching any sort of moral conduct since this preaching assumed that people could be good by an act of the will. We were made good only by the grace of God and the extent to which we submitted to it. As a Buddhist friend and contemporary (a former Christian) once said to me, "The trouble with Christianity is that it doesn't teach you how to be good."

To meet this theology, an Episcopal priest named Reuel Howe wrote a book called *Man's Need and God's Action* (Greenwich, CT: Seabury Press, 1953). This book, which came straight out of counseling theory and clinical pastoral education, did not deny the agape doctrine of God's love for human beings, but it saw all human love as evidence of God's love and human community as the most reliable channel of and witness to this love. The human need for God's love is all-acceptable, indeed a given part of being human, and God's love comes to meet this need through other human beings. God's love depends on human love for its expression and comes as an answer to human need, not in spite of human sin. Howe's doctrine of love was a blending of agape and eros with a new injection of humanism—a mixture of Tillich and Buber and Howe. *Man's Need and God's Action* was a good book, which anyone could read and most Episcopalians did. It gave consistency to preaching in Episcopal churches for a decade.

Superficially understood, this theology lent itself too easily to a theology of counseling theory. The theological dimensions of the book were either trivialized or forgotten in many parishes, resulting in a heavy accent on community as an expression of human love in the name of Christ, a kind of minimalist Christianity. In some cases this further evolved into a kind of human potential, I'm-okay-you're-okay health spa masquerading as a parish. In others, a basically valid and serious Christianity was watered down, and preaching became a series of self-help lectures with an orthodox Christian postscript. Preachers had trouble finding a way to preach the Gospel with any power that did not depend on assaulting the self-esteem of their parishioners.

Is There a Middle Way?

Now let me suggest a preaching theology which contains both a biblical edge and insights from counseling theory, one that helps people alter their behavior while maintaining their self-esteem.

First of all, some basic theological assumptions. Human beings are made in the image of God, but their consciousness of their mortality, their knowledge of the difference between themselves as creatures and God their creator makes them captive to Satan, to the fear of death. Sin, then, is this captivity, this bondage. It is nothing inherently evil in ourselves. The power of sin lies in our consciousness of our mortality and of ourselves; we alone of the creation possess it. What is most God-like about us is also what causes us to sin. What frees us from our DNA makes us the captives of language and culture, removing us from the rest of creation by giving us dominion over it and stewardship of it.

Language, the command of the word, gives us power; our power to name gives us a certain ability to control. But at the same time the word, the symbol is not the thing; the map is not the territory; and our view of reality is distorted at all times by our exaggerated need to exploit reality to assure our own survival, even if it is at the expense of the survival of others. This is the nature of our bondage, our sin. It is not of our essence, not at the heart of the self, where we are like God.

The atonement, what Jesus accomplished in reconciling us to himself, lay in becoming one of us, perfectly human (that is, perfectly imperfect), and acting as a person free to love even at the risk of death, ignoring the claims of Satan even though he, like us, was mortal and subject to the same mortal fate of suffering and death. Through the cross Jesus overcame the power of death. The very consciousness of death which kept us in its bondage, when touched by the word understood as Jesus Christ, can become consciousness of resurrection and eternal life as the final end of the divine-human enterprise. Sacrificial love, love that makes holy by risking and spending itself, overcomes the kingdom of death, the rule of entropy, and frees the human race from its bondage of fear.

Working from this theology, one never in a prophetic frenzy attacks persons or groups. One speaks harshly and negatively only of specific behavior, or specific examples of bad thinking leading directly to hateful destructive behavior. Martin Luther King seldom attacked particular people or even broad ideologies; he seldom if ever attacked racism. But King was relentless in his attack on racial discrimination, an ideology which (like apartheid) leads directly to whole patterns of behavior that derive from fear. Segregation, racial discrimination, violence, ignoring of the law—all these forms of *behavior* were the focus of King's prophetic wrath.

With this theology one never attacks feelings or tells people how they ought to feel. Feelings are spontaneous; they are not voluntary, unlike behavior. When we attack racism, white people who either dislike or fear people of color feel personally attacked, because they cannot change their feelings on demand. They can, however, change their behavior. And there is considerable evidence that attitudinal change follows behavioral change rather than precedes it. This is old wisdom and a part of classical Christian ethics. Because ethically we are responsible only for our behavior and not for our feelings, we must never in preaching or praying tell people how they are "supposed" to feel or tell them what it is bad to feel.

Nor do we threaten people by saying that this or that is a question of survival, whether the issue is the parish's every member canvass or the passage of a bill in Congress. Whatever the case, the threat to survival doesn't motivate: either it depresses people and causes apathy or else it causes impulsively defensive behavior—especially if their self-esteem is at a level where they believe that they deserve to die. All such allusions to survival, or winning, or success, are made under the authority of sin-and-death, the reign of Satan.

When preaching from this theology (which shares something with Reinhold Niebuhr, William Stringfellow, and Martin Luther King), one is able to preach the choice of conversion to Jesus Christ not as salvation from being evil and sinful to becoming good, nor from anxiety and alienation to acceptance and belonging, but from captivity to freedom. It is a freedom that honors the next choice: to join in the corporate task of sanctification by participating to whatever degree in the building of a moral world.

In a rapidly changing world that seems to drive people into increasingly self-protective measures, perhaps the crucial first step for all serious Christians is to go beyond the belief that any choice which does not immediately serve our own survival is neurotic and self-deceptive. This, of course, is the message of the Gospel: perfect love casts out fear. It relieves the fear of death and failure, embarrassment and error. Where our preaching can move beyond the survival aims of therapeutic theory to salvation from the bondage of sin and death, maintaining and building upon the inherent worth of the individual, then we have a basis for preaching as the very architecture of a moral world.

Notes:

1. Perhaps this is why I have never liked Paul very much. As one immersed in the language and habits of the therapeutic culture, I see Paul as an arrogant and often moralistic man telling me how to act and what to believe. Yet, unlike the preacher I heard on my vacation, he never tells me who I am and then says that who I am is unacceptable. Any sermon that focuses on my presumed personality type rather than my behavior is merely scolding; it may make me feel vaguely miserable, but it will not help me change my behavior. Paul's metaphor of milk and meat, on the other hand, suggests to me that the behavior can be outgrown. The biblical image implies a freedom to change, the possibility of true metanoia as a slow, intentional, developmental process.

2. Given the range of positions on many issues, stewardship of both time and money is one of the few aspects of moral behavior in the parish about which there is still some consensus. Although the rationale for this consensus is more often based on survival than salvation, stewardship is a truly moral issue. It is a metaphor and a sacramental expression of mutual concern within the body of Christ.

3. Another assumption goes along with this—that talking of successful therapy presupposes clients whose basic trust is intact, whose pathology does not occur at such a deep level. A psychoanalyst like Hans Kohut maintains that in treating disorder stemming from damage at this level of trust, one must work out strategies that avoid getting into this deepest and best defended level of the unconscious. Otherwise, the

therapy can be more dangerous to the patient than the defenses themselves. I have even heard a Jesuit spiritual director say that a person damaged at this trust level can never really learn to pray. I think this is silly, but I would agree that it is dangerous to expect people whose ego isn't in very good shape to practice a mode of prayer which demands the obliteration of the ego. Whether this form of prayer, common to Tibetan Buddhism, is an appropriate form of Christian prayer is something which should be examined more closely than I think it has been.

4. According to Bruno Bettelheim, the German word translated into the English word "ego" really means "soul"—not some sharp-eyed, objective, scientific core of personality, but the unique whole of a person in balance.

5. Agape was shoved down our throats in seminary. The important thing, the dean told me, was the purification of the motive, by which he meant getting every bit of eros out of our agape until it was clean as a whistle. Yet this involved a contradiction: the very attempt to rid our agape of eros was obviously either an erotic or a nomic process, an attempt to save ourselves by works. The place of prayer in agape was logically unclear if it went beyond asking God to do what it was God's nature to do anyway. Certainly we didn't seek God's companionship; God had already sought out ours.

Preaching and Inclusiveness

Patricia Wilson-Kastner

"How are they [Jews and Gentiles] to hear without someone to proclaim Christ?" (Romans 10:14–17). Paul, in his consideration of the redemption of all people, Jews and Gentiles alike, raises the necessity of preachers proclaiming the Gospel to all people so that they can hear and believe. We today, in our electronic, pluralistic age, have to consider the same basic question. What does it mean to preach the Gospel to all people? How can we preach the Gospel to all people? Why preach the Gospel to all people?

These interconnected questions are deep and wide, and become further complicated when we remember that we are not just, as Karl Barth's famous metaphor about preaching suggests, throwing stones and wondering who they will hit. Preaching is an effort to communicate with other humans. In a liturgy, the preacher explores with a community of faith the relationship between the Word of God and our present-day lives—individual and corporate. In this process, the intention of the preacher as preacher is not just to reach this or that small group of people, but to be a part of that great voice of the communion of saints which utters the apostolic faith in its own day and age and invites the world to respond.

Preaching and Inclusiveness

The apostle Paul, in applying Psalm 19 to the preacher's task, quotes: "their voice has gone out to all the earth, and their word to the ends of the world." From the very beginning of Christian preaching, a tension abides in the very roots of preaching itself. The scope of Christian preaching is wider than just a sermon to one group at one time. Preaching is a liturgical prayer, a remembering, an *anamnesis*, of the Scripture as it relates to the life of a specific Christian community as a part of the body of Christ. It recalls what God *has* done in order to cast light on what God *is* doing among us, and on what God calls us to *become*. Preaching is thus both very particular and very universal in its aim: in it the Word of God is proclaimed to *this* congregation, at the same time affirming that the Word of God is intended for *all* people.

Preaching thus always begins with a specific preacher at one time and place addressing a congregation of certain identifiable individuals with their own histories. At the same time, it directs us to a universal temporal and spatial fulfillment of God's love for the world. This tension between being chosen/particularity and inclusiveness/universality is deep in the Scriptures. The book of Ruth on the one hand and the strictures of Ezra on the other testify to the struggle. Christianity tips the balance in the Hebrew Scriptures definitively towards universality and inclusiveness (e.g., John 12:35-37, Romans 8). The dynamic of Christian preaching pushes out towards the horizon of the whole world, both in those preached to and the message proclaimed. Gospel preaching thus always speaks with a missionary voice. In this sense preaching is always inclusive, seeking to draw all to God by proclaiming the Gospel to all. But what is "inclusiveness"? It has become a buzzword lately, but its meaning is not always clear.

Does preaching's desire to be universal grow from an urge to proclaim exactly the same message everywhere, with the desire to have everyone think, act, and feel in the same way? Everyone is welcome, such preaching proclaims, but only if they believe and behave in precisely the same way. One might preach the same sermon in 3rd century Jerusalem or 20th century Rio de Janeiro, and expect adherence to the same beliefs and moral code by all Christians everywhere at all times. If the apostle Paul said that women should be silent in church in the presence of their husbands, and slaves respect their owners, that behavior is a universal law for Christians. God expects everyone, everywhere, to be the same. That sort of inclusiveness does admit everyone, but at the price of individuality, cultural integrity, and acceptance of the historical character of the Bible and divine Revelation.

On the other hand, is inclusiveness an intention to reach out to everyone with some message about God or Jesus, with no particular attention to whether there is a congruence or similarity between Gospel words and human behavior? In this case, the only aim of preaching would be to convince everyone to take the name of Christian, and accept everyone else who wished as a Christian, with no attention to the content of Christianity. This approach would be an absolutely tolerant religious pluralism. For instance, I may preach to a congregation of gay Christians in contemporary Amsterdam that Jesus loves them, and preach the same message to Xhosa liberation fighters in South Africa. The preacher's only concern would be that both congregations give allegiance to the figure of Jesus as one they admire and respect. Their behavior is irrelevant.

What Is Inclusiveness?

This question has been raised in many forms during the history of Christianity. For instance, in the seventeenth century the Chinese Rites controversy pressed the Church to ask whether the Gospel could be truly proclaimed and lived if ideas from Confucianism were used about the Christian God and if such customs as ancestor worship were observed in modified form.[1] Today we in the United States are more concerned with issues of inclusive language and whether active gays and lesbians can be Christians. In other places analogous queries are raised: can groups pledged to violence, such as the Sinn Fein, be considered Christians in good standing? Is armed resistance by blacks in South Africa a morally legitimate and even necessary choice? Where are the borders of acceptance? What are the boundaries, beyond which no one or no more can be included? Does the universe created and governed by God have its limits?

The origins of the word "inclusive" suggest that the situation is more complex than first meets the eye or the imagination. The roots are Latin: "in" *in* and "claudere" *to shut up*. Inclusiveness is not, at its roots, a blanket validation of everything, but rather begins with a notion of setting boundaries and borders, and then expands to the drawing in of smaller individuals, parts, or categories, into a greater whole. The assumption, at least in the root sense of inclusivity, is that the whole into which others are being included has a clear identity and integrity. Others are brought, invited, or belong within its greater comprehensiveness.

Thus for the preacher, inclusiveness involves identifying both the greater unity/whole into which people are being invited (or already belong) and the individuals and parts who are being invited. It also involves communicating in such a way that people receive the message of inclusivity, of invitation, of belonging. This task sounds complicated, and in our present pluralistic society, it is.

If we follow the previous approach to inclusiveness, it does not mean saying: "Everything is OK and we are all OK because everything is OK." Nor does inclusiveness mean proclaiming: "God's realm is intended for all creation, but only people of specific genders or sexuality or intelligence can enter as first class citizens." Inclusiveness involves proclaiming clearly the core of God's Good News: the realm of God's justice and love is come to earth, in creation, through the incarnation, and through our transformation in the spirit of God. *Who is invited to enter in? Everyone and everything.* At no cost? Just everyone come? Is that inclusiveness? "Yes," we respond, "and no."

Yes, in the sense that God created all the world and intends to redeem all the world (e.g., Psalm 100, Romans 8:18–23, 1 Corinthians 15:28). We are accepted by God, according to the Christian vision, not because we have earned it, but because God freely loves us (Galatians 2:6). God's redemptive love embraces every-thing and everyone. But *no*, entry into God's realm of justice and love also costs, because the one who freely enters thereby chooses to conform him or herself to God's realm (e.g. Deuteronomy 5–6, John 3:16, Philippians 2:1–13). Even with a superficial glance at the Scriptures, the shape of inclusiveness draws together both a uni-versal vision in which all are brought together in God, and borders and boundaries of this realm of divine love.

Inclusiveness is, for the Christian preacher, the invitation to all people to come and eat at God's table and be part of God's community. Thus proclaiming the nature of inclusiveness involves careful attention and balance between the invitation freely offered to all people to enter the realm of God's love, embodied in the church, and an insistence on the very real bounds of God's realm and the cost involved in our entering into it.

God's Realm

We must begin with the Biblical notion of the realm[2] which is the foundation and raison d'etre of inclusiveness. "Behold the reign of God is at hand, repent and believe in the Good News." Thus, according to the Gospels, John the Baptist preached, and so also Jesus himself. God's realm is absolute, total, cosmic. It is also utterly inclusive. The aim of preaching such a Gospel is to draw all people into a realm of God in which the universal justice of God governs everyone and everything.

The Scriptures assume that the world and all its creatures are created in justice, and God is coming to judge the world in justice (e.g. Psalm 96:10–14). That is, God will restore the original right relationships between God and the world, and among all creatures. In this realm God's steadfast and faithful love undergirds and animates the divine justice governing the world and God's actions in it (Psalm 136). The preaching of the Christian Gospel alerts people that in and through Jesus Christ God's judgment and justice are now active in the world to inaugurate and bring to birth the realm of God on this earth, here and now (Mark 1:14, John

5:19–29, Acts 2:14–36). Thus the realm of God is willed by God to include all creation.

To explore the realm of God is to point to the core of Christian preaching, even though in a short space one can scarcely claim fully to explore it.[3] The essence of my comments is that the Christian claim is utterly inclusive in the sense of intending to bring everything into God's realm of justice and love. Because God created everything, everything is intended to be an integral part of God's realm. Jesus' person and ministry are intended to restore the interconnections which are at the heart of creation and weave it together with God's self.

Nothing is exempted or excluded from God's realm. The Scripture knows no First Amendment distinction between religion and state, or scholarly division between secular and profane. A realm of God which does not include everything is deficient or lacking. God is sovereign over all. Paul's great vision in 1 Corinthians 15:28 regards Christ's lordship as finding its fulfillment in the ultimate sovereignty of God, who will be all in all.

The Biblical vision of inclusiveness has been articulated by different preachers in this century, from diverse perspectives. For instance, Christine M. Smith, from an explicitly feminist perspective, uses weaving as a central metaphor for preaching because she understands Christianity to be primarily concerned with weaving together concerns for global peace and justice, commitment to practice and action in order to transform and reshape the whole world.[4] She, like most feminist theologians, rejects any distinction between politics and religion, and regards the concerns of Christianity to be holistic, in the sense of seeking the good of the entire human being, as a part of the whole human race, as a part of the earth. All is, and must be, included among those invited into and made a part of the universe Christianity affirms in God's name.

From a different Christian viewpoint, in his opening address to Lambeth Conference 1988, Archbishop Robert Runcie identified the vision from the book of Revelation of the new heaven and the new earth, "God's disclosure of the unity of the whole human family."[5] For Runcie God's agenda for the world is "shalom, unity and communion."[6] In this context we strive for the kingdom of

God on earth, which can never be identified with any particular political agenda. Furthermore, as part of the task of the church we extend this notion of unity in God's shalom to the whole of creation. In Christ we find our renewal: it is the "task of the one Church of Jesus Christ to embody more visibly this new humanity as Good News for all people and all creation."[7] The primary goal of the church is thus to proclaim and promote the healing of all in God through Christ.

Inclusiveness: What Does It Require?

These visions of inclusiveness are but two of many contemporary reworkings of the Biblical notion of the inclusion of all creation in God's reign. Many questions about inclusiveness could and ought to be asked of these and other efforts: about their roots in tradition, openness to the present and future, their comprehensiveness, relation to the claims of other religions, etc. But the preacher must take up a more immediate task, which requires asking about the borders and the boundaries of inclusiveness, the cost of entering into God's realm. Because preaching connects God and religious values with everyday life, it is urgent that we answer the question of how God's inclusiveness demands that we live.

In other words, how do we move from our present condition towards the fullness of the realm of God? When inviting people to "seek the realm of God above all else," what are we asking them to do? Is inclusiveness just another cover for uniformity, in which everyone is invited to become part of a whole in which all the parts are expected to be identical? Or, from the other extreme, is anything acceptable for those who enter into God's inclusive realm? What does it look like and act like to be included in God's realm? In short, the preacher must seek for an ethic of inclusiveness, and proclaim this ethic along with the vision of God's reign among us.

In a careful and provocative study of sexual ethics in the Bible, L. William Countryman has raised certain questions which are relevant to the issue of inclusiveness. He makes a very strong case that Old and New Testament sexual ethics cannot be directly transformed and followed in today's world, because "they are formed in terms of purity and property systems that no longer prevail among us."[8] Instead of concluding that Christian sexual ethics are irrelevant, he suggests that instead we must, in our own day, apply the Biblical values and critique to sexual institutions "on behalf of the Gospel of God's grace."[9]

Countryman's approach is equally applicable to our effort to look for an ethics of inclusiveness. We must clarify our own understanding of inclusiveness and God's realm, and apply it to the institutions of inclusiveness and exclusiveness in our own time. The preacher is thus called on to be the prophet of God's inclusiveness to the world. The following are some of the principles which the preacher may find helpful in the task.

1) *Being included into the realm of God is an act of divine grace, not human merit.* We are invited into God's realm because God created us, dwelt among us, and loves us. Thus, no human being can count out or include another in God's name. This is an essential starting point, because the fundamental human urge is for us to set boundaries, and be gatekeepers into the realm of God. The Gospel assures us that God alone sets the terms for the divine realm on earth, and for our belonging to that realm.

2) *Inclusiveness involves coming into God's realm, not the place or situation of our own devising.* Consequently, every social system, value, process, and each individual need to be judged by the dynamics of God's realm. The question is never "how do I get what I want?" or "how do I set the borders of God's realm?" but "how can I be obedient to God's call? how can I conform myself to Christ?" The root religious attitude is openness to God for oneself, not judgment of what God asks others to do, and how I ought to pass judgment on them.

3) *The human motivation for inclusiveness is our desire to be interconnected and included within the greater whole of God's creation.* Desire has often been downplayed or rejected as unworthy in postbiblical Christianity, and yet the language of Scripture is full of the language of longing, desire, wanting, waiting, hoping. Inclusiveness, becoming part of God's realm, is a powerful image because we human beings passionately want more than our fractious and fragmentary selves can provide. We want to be part of the whole cosmos, and to draw others with us. Eros attracts us to God, and to interconnection with everything else in God.

4) *The ethics of inclusiveness are founded in God's love.* We want to be part of the whole, the realm of all things in God. The name of that interconnectedness, and the name of God in whom all exists, is love (1 John 4:16). Consequently, every thought, every action of individual or community, must be assessed on whether it grows from love and promotes the growth of the world in love. For instance, do we treat others as equal citizens of God's realm? Do we pray with and for them in that light? Of course, specific situations have their own complexities and people their mixed motives, but at the center is always God's love for all creation.

5) *A missionary dynamic is an essential element of all preaching.* I do not mean that we are always to be telling people to join the church, but that as preachers we are called to spread the message of God's realm on earth as widely as possible. Preaching which is primarily concerned with in-house church issues, fosters self-congratulation, promotes selected moral issues to the exclusion of other broader ones, or focuses on psychological self-help, is not Christian preaching because it does not have at its center the invitation to everyone to be part of God's realm.

6) *Discipline in God's earthly realm is intended to prevent us from hurting or excluding others.* When ought the preacher to condemn behavior or forbid it in God's name? Discipline in the church or the wider community is never intended to exclude another, from the church or the realm of God. However, if someone is excluding or hurting them in their efforts to be faithful members of God's realm, it is essential to the health of the life of love in God's realm that such persons be restrained from damaging others. Love and inclusiveness demand limits on behavior as well as the encouragement and nurture of the good.

Conclusion

These observations and suggestions merely touch on some issues of inclusivity and preaching. Besides a deeper treatment of the issues already raised, others must be addressed: language about God and humanity in preaching, the relationship between Christianity and other religions, the relation of preaching to the rest of the liturgy, responding to the challenges and needs of specific congregations, etc. I trust, however, that the brief comments here offer a theological opening for continuing dialogue.

Notes:

1. John McManners, "The Expansion of Christianity," in *The Oxford Illustrated History of Christianity*, ed. John McManners (Oxford: University Press, 1990), pp. 325–328.

2. *malkuth Yahweh, basileia tou theou.* The most common English translation is "kingdom." To avoid simple identification of God's dominion on earth with one specific place, and to eschew sexism, other terms are more commonly being used today: realm, reign, dominion. I have chosen to use "realm" because it seems to me to preserve the notion of a real sovereignty of God on earth, related to but not identified with the social and political world.

3. Frederick H. Borsch, *Many Things in Parables* (Philadelphia: Fortress, 1988); John Bright, *The Kingdom of God* (Nashville: Abington, 1953); C. H. Dodd, *The Parables of the Kingdom* (New York: Charles Scribners, 1961); John R. Donahue, *The Gospel in Parable* (Philadelphia: Fortress, 1988).

4. Christine M. Smith, *Weaving the Sermon* (Louisville: Westminster/John Knox, 1989), pp. 105–138.

5. Robert Runcie, "The Nature of the Unity We Seek," in *The Truth Shall Make You Free: The Lambeth Conference 1988* (London: Church House Publishing [for the Anglican Consultative Council], 1988), p. 11.

6. *Idem.*

7. *Ibid,* pp. 22–24.

8. L. William Countryman, *Dirt, Greed, & Sex* (Philadelphia: Fortress, 1988), p. 237. Krister Stendahl, *The Bible and the Role of Women* (Philadelphia: Fortress, 1966), pp. 18–24, explores the same issue of the "translatibility" of the Scriptures to the contemporary world.

9. Countryman, p. 239.

Preaching and the Prayers of the People

Carl P. Daw, Jr.

WHEN ASKED THE DIFFERENCE between preaching and praying, an eager church school student is said to have blurted out, "Preaching is telling people off, and prayer is telling God off." Whether the story is actual or apocryphal, its caricature of our assumptions is very revealing, especially its implication that both situations are expected to be adversarial. It also shows how much work remains to be done in encouraging those who preach and those who lead prayers to recognize and embrace their common challenge to help a congregation open themselves to seek and do God's will.

How Is Prayer Related to Preaching?

It is a commonplace of homiletic handbooks and instruction that prayer should precede and inform every aspect of sermon preparation. Such received wisdom is ratified by every preacher's experience. But, like too many of our other assumptions about prayer, it is generally treated as a private and preliminary aspect of preaching rather than an integral component or desired outcome. In the past, when the liturgy or local custom expected a hymn immediately before the sermon, preachers often left the singing of the last few stanzas to the congregation and choir and knelt for private prayer before entering the pulpit. In many places there is still a kind of vestigial "prayer before sermon," most commonly some form of Trinitarian invocation. Yet even these actions and words in the midst of the worshiping assembly have generally reinforced the attitude that prayer is something to be done *before* rather than *during* the sermon: a sort of spiritual handwashing or ritual cleansing.

Though such disjointedness in liturgy manifests itself in numerous ways, I believe that it ultimately derives from a failure to understand worship as corporate prayer. This, in turn, is a symptom of the assumption that prayer is always entreaty, a constant attempt to persuade God to do what we believe to be best. The catechism clearly teaches that, on the contrary, prayer is "responding to God, by thought and by deeds, with or without words" and further notes that "the principal kinds of prayer are adoration, praise, thanksgiving, penitence, oblation, intercession, and petition," each of which is then defined (BCP, pp. 856–857). But the experience of most worshipers reinforces the attitude that praying involves asking God for something. How often, for example, awkward silence follows the bidding to thank God "for all the blessings of this life" (BCP, p. 393).[1] Such silence is also evidence that our focus has become so habitually individualistic that we lose sight of what it means truly to pray as the Body of Christ. One of the neglected missions of preaching is to foster a corporate awareness of how we can seek and respond to God's will by hearing and receiving God's word.

It is both ironic and sad that the structural centrality of prayer in our rites is not experienced as such. Especially in the Eucharist, "the principal act of Christian worship on the Lord's Day and other major Feasts" (BCP, p. 13), the Prayers of the People are frequently treated as an awkward but necessary transition between the Liturgy of the Word and the Liturgy of the Table, rather like a utilitarian corridor between two festive rooms. Though we have learned how to provide continuity to our worship through careful

Carl P. Daw, Jr.   193

coordination of music and eucharistic prayers and seasonal blessings with the appointed propers, we seldom devote the same care to the Prayers of the People. It is still not widely recognized—even among clergy and others who plan worship—that the rubrics do *not* require the use of any of the forms of prayer in the Prayer Book. All that is required in either Rite I or Rite II is that the Prayers of the People include six specified topics of intercession (BCP, pp. 328, 383). The forms provided are models of how the prayers may be offered, but they are not indispensable.[2] The freedom to adapt or write prayers for use in a particular congregation on a specific occasion is also a challenge to integrate the elements of that liturgy so that Word, Sacrament, and People unite in a living sacrifice of praise and thanksgiving.

Such prayerful unity is not decorative or superficial. Nor does it happen by coincidence or accident. Careful, reverent, and attentive preparation is needed in order to discover the thread—or perhaps more accurately the web—of connection among the day or season, the propers, the people, and the place. Like any other faithful search, such revelation is more likely to occur if it is done in community than if it is done by individuals working alone. There is simply no substitute for having several people involved in the process. Though it may often seem time-consuming and inefficient, such collaborative preparation done in a spirit of prayer and mutual exploration will stabilize and nourish worship just as a strong root system allows a great tree to flourish. The cumulative effect of such unified worship will both exemplify and foster a spirit of corporate engagement; where the parts of the service complement and serve each other, they help the worshipers to find and claim their own interconnections within the Body of Christ as well as their ministry and mission in the world.

Such prayer-permeated worship should not be dismissed as idealistic and unrealistic. Quite the opposite, it is inextricably grounded in reality. The late Rachel Hosmer, O.S.H., used to tell her classes in ascetics: "The problem with most people who claim their prayers are not answered is that they pray from somewhere they are not, but where they think they are supposed to be. Yet God is faithful and always responds to the place we prayed from, and we're not there to hear the answer." Prayerful worship—including prayerful preaching—calls us to be both firmly rooted and deeply honest. Like the medieval stonecarvers who carefully sculpted the tops of the gargoyles that could not be seen by people on the ground, those who prepare and conduct such worship do so not for aesthetic or utilitarian reasons but because they seek to offer God their best efforts. Prayerful preaching therefore requires skill, wisdom, dedication, and sheer hard work in order to connect the will of God revealed through scripture and tradition with the joys and sorrows of the congregation for whom it is delivered.

Preaching the Intercessions

Some idea of how this approach might be put into practice can be suggested by considering possible connections between the specified intercession of the Prayers of the People and what is said in the sermon.

Prayer for "the Universal Church, its members, and its mission" offers an almost endless store of opportunities for the preacher. This first intercession reminds us of our baptism into and affirmation of the "one holy catholic and apostolic Church" rather than into any denomination or parish. If such a prayer informs how other Christians—both local and global—are characterized in sermons as well as how other Episcopalians are mentioned, there will be no room for the rancor and suspicion that have too often infected the pulpit. This very comprehensive petition also reminds us that the preacher has almost endless opportunities to offer specific instances of ways our common life in the whole Body of Christ is enhanced by its various members. For example, the insights of the Eastern Orthodox Churches often provide a helpful counterpoint to the interpretations traditional in Western Christianity. Alternatively, some aspect of the life and practice of the portion of the Anglican Communion being remembered in the Anglican Cycle of Prayer that day may offer a fresh perspective on the appointed Gospel. Similarly, prayer for the members of the Church Universal invites us to recall and celebrate that incredibly diverse company of saints—past, present, and future—through whom we catch renewed glimmers of God's grace. This is an invitation to remind ourselves that God's pattern of revelation is always incarnational: it happens in and through human beings. Which leads unavoidably to the mission God has entrusted to the Church both corporately and individually to proclaim by word and deed the good news of God's love made known in Jesus Christ. To paraphrase Paul, "how can we pray for these things if we do not preach them?"

The direction to pray for "the Nation and all in authority" is a two-edged sword that the preacher must wield with great care. On the one hand, we are indeed blessed to live in a land where religious freedom is assured and where most people enjoy a quality of life only dreamt of in other parts of the world. We can truly rejoice for the opportunities these advantages give us in bearing witness to our faith. But we need to extricate ourselves from too cozy an identification of Christian faith and practice with "the American way." In particular, we need to remember that we are Christians first and Americans (or anything else) second. As Paul admonished the Philippians long ago, Stanley Hauerwas and William Willimon have recently reminded us that we are "resident aliens" whose true homeland is not of this world.[3] We still have much work to do in making this clear in many parishes where the American flag stands in the church (sometimes even in the chancel) or is carried in procession. In this regard our Roman Catholic neighbors are to be emulated in their recognition that "identifying symbols of particular cultures, groups, or nations are not appropriate as permanent parts of the liturgical environment."[4] To proclaim the ultimate sovereignty of God and truly to pray "your kingdom come, your will be done, on earth as in heaven" will not be popular when the full implications of such preaching and prayers are realized. But it is precisely in the hope for the revelation of God's sovereignty that we dare to pray for those in civil authority: we pray for human justice and peace as incomplete anticipations of God's reign of mercy and shalom.

To pray for "the welfare of the world" is not simply a longing for peace, health, and prosperity for all people but also involves a recognition of our stewardship of creation and our vital connection with all parts of "this fragile earth, our island home" (BCP, p. 370). It is an affirmation of our confidence that "the creation itself will be set free from its bondage to decay and will obtain the freedom of the glory of the children of God" (Romans 8:21). The barrage of media-borne information about the world's needs threatens to overwhelm us, to make us despair of ever doing anything about hunger, poverty, disease, war, violence, degradation, abuse, greed, corruption, ignorance, waste, depletion of resources, drought, global warming, and a host of other problems. We are called both to proclaim that God "does not willingly afflict or grieve anyone" (Lamentations 3:33) and to pray "not only with our lips, but in our lives" (BCP, pp. 59, 72, 101, 125) by doing all we can to promote the welfare of the world. By using water for Baptism, bread and wine for Eucharist, and oil for anointing, sacramental worship affirms both the salvific potential of all creation and the reality that God in Christ has already set us free from the bondage of sin and death. This truth and this hope need to be proclaimed from the pulpit as well: the welfare of the world is not something we attempt against a malevolent and intractable God but with and for a loving and sustaining God.

Prayers for "the concerns of the local community" are a good barometer of the connection between our faith and our lives. It is both scandalous and amusing how separate we try to keep what we do on Sunday morning from what we do the rest of the week. Do we really believe that God neither knows or cares? No less serious is the fear of social consequences that renders Christians reluctant to seek and offer mutual help. We are still too caught in the traps of "what will people think?" and "will I lose face?" Another hindrance to open and honest prayer is its misuse as an occasion to impose our views—even our good intentions—on others. During my orientation week at seminary, the dean warned our entering class that "in this chapel, no one is to commit prayer against anyone else." That memorable phrase effectively reminded us that prayer is not a time to grind axes or settle scores. Nor is it a time to make news releases: if there has been a death or illness or accident that most of the congregation will not yet know about, something should be said before the prayers begin. It is not a bad idea to ask routinely, "Are there any announcements that need to be made to inform our prayers?" Such a practice allows information to be communicated to other worshipers directly (thus avoiding prayers which imply that God is ignorant of certain details) and also encourages more people to support this concern in their prayers. The ability and willingness of those who preach and those who lead prayers to model appropriate interaction between worship and daily life will do much to encourage prayerful participation by the congregation, both silently and aloud. Preachers should not shrink from talking about our need to bring our honest concerns before God in prayer as well as our need to be open to the discovery of God's will. As Jesus reminded his disciples when healing the man born blind, that impairment was not a punishment for sin but an opportunity for God's glory to be manifest (John 9:3). Both in our preaching and our praying, it is essential to remain open to the possibility that what we perceive as disaster and defeat may be precisely the place where God is seeking to do a new thing in and through us.

No portion of the Prayers of the People elicits more frequent or heartfelt participation than the intercessions for "those who suffer and those in any trouble." To a significant extent this is learned behavior, reinforced by the place for congregational intercessions in several of our forms of prayer. The prayer "for the whole state of Christ's Church and the world," for example, permits "additional prayers and thanksgivings" immediately after reminding us of "all those who, in this transitory life, are in trouble, sorrow, need sickness, or any other adversity" (BCP, pp. 329–330).[5] Similarly, Form III invites the congregation to offer additional prayers by bidding, "Let us pray for our own *needs* and those of others" (BCP, p. 387; emphasis added). This liturgical emphasis on petition and intercession seems further strengthened by the lectionary, which shows a tendency to preface gospels on prayer with readings describing Abraham bargaining with God for the preservation of Sodom, or Jacob wrestling with God at the Jabbok.[6] Preachers have the opportunity to help congregations recognize the divine good will that both precedes and motivates human entreaty, as well as the dangers of spiritual pride if we credit ourselves with changing God's mind.

Prayers for the departed are not simply sanctified nostalgia. As people who believe that there is life beyond physical death, we affirm that God continues to care for those who have entered into another realm of life. As the Catechism declares, "we trust that in God's presence those who have chosen to serve him will grow in his love, until they see him as he is" (BCP, p. 862). We therefore remember before God "all who have died in the peace of Christ, and those whose faith is known to [God] alone" (BCP, p. 375). It is also important to recognize that, like all prayer, this is not a one-way street. We not only remember those who have died; we can also ask their prayers for us, in much the same way that we might ask anyone else to pray for us. Unfortunately, neither of these requests feels very comfortable for us, and even clergy often feel awkward in addressing this subject. But anyone who has been through the death of someone close can testify to an awareness of personal presence that transcends memory. Such moments are almost too precious to recount, yet they are far more common than we imagine. These fleeting foretastes of resurrection are the experiences we have ritualized into our calendar of holy days. Especially those commemorations that make up the Lesser Feasts and Fasts connect us with myriad expressions of the Paschal Mystery and diverse testimonies to Christ's Resurrection—and to our own. Both as a preparation for the Prayers of the People at each Eucharist and as a foundation for dealing with death (whether their own or another's), congregations need to hear these themes mentioned in sermons as a regular matter of course. Trying to tie up all the loose ends in a funeral sermon will be too little too late.

While a series of sermons organized around the rubrical intercessions of the Prayers of the People might yield an effective Lenten Preaching Mission or other special cycle, it would be an inappropriate substitute for the faithful proclamation of each Sunday's appointed scriptures. In fact, a more effective approach in the long run will be to include these matters in sermons regularly without making them the principal subject. The cumulative effect of a preacher's recurring convictions often proves more persuasive

Carl P. Daw, Jr.

and more enduring than an occasional full-dress sermon concentrating on a few of them. Even for the most devout and eloquent homilist, that such prayers are taken seriously will be communicated better by practice than by preaching.

What about Other Kinds of Prayer?

Although the rubrical requirements for the Prayers of the People all concern intercession and petition, two of the forms provided (II and VI) explicitly offer opportunity for thanksgivings, and Form VI can conclude with penitence through the use of an alternative confession.[7] Otherwise, there is no provision for adoration, praise, or oblation. These deficiencies can sometimes be offset by the celebrant's choice of collect at the conclusion of the prayers. Also, allowing a significant period of silence before that collect provides an opportunity for adoration—the quiet enjoyment of the presence of God, for which the unburdening of petition and intercession may be a conducive preparation.[8]

But it will probably be more helpful to recognize that prayer is not limited to the portion of the liturgy we call the Prayers of the People. Even a cursory review of the shape of the liturgy makes this clear. Near the beginning of the service, the Collect of the Day provides us with a context for hearing the appointed scriptures.[9] Then at various points we sing psalms, canticles, and hymns—both metrical hymns chosen for the day and the central angelic hymn of the liturgy, the Sanctus. In doing so we experience the wisdom of Augustine's remark long ago, "Whoever sings, prays twice." The second half of the liturgy opens with The Great Thanksgiving expressed in various Eucharistic Prayers leading to the Lord's Prayer, and we conclude the Holy Communion with a Postcommunion Prayer. In short, prayer is the essence of worship, not something added on or optional.

If preaching aims to be an integral part of worship, it must also partake of this prayerful attitude.[10] Such proclamation is offered not as a new word but as the faithful response, the authentic echo, to God's own word to us. That word will not return empty, but will accomplish what God has intended (Isaiah 55:11). So we believe, and so we preach.

Notes:

1. On the other hand, silence is preferable to "thanksgivings" that are insensitive to the situations of other worshippers. To give thanks for one's prosperity while standing beside someone who is unemployed or for one's happy family life when the person in the next pew is going through a difficult divorce is little more than sanctified selfishness.

2. See the discussion of the Prayers of the People in *Supplemental Liturgical Materials* (New York: Church Hymnal Corporation, 1991), pp. 33–34.

3. *Resident Aliens* (Nashville: Abingdon Press, 1989); cf. Philippians 2:5–11, 3:20–21.

4. Bishops' Committee on the Liturgy, *Environment and Art in Catholic Worship* (Washington, DC: United States Catholic Conference, 1978), par. 101. I have even heard one prominent Roman Catholic liturgical writer remark that this prohibition would include the Vatican flag!

5. It should be noted that this prayer is prefaced by a rarely-used rubric authorizing "an appropriate response" by the congregation after each paragraph. Although Marion Hatchett suggests a recurring response (*Commentary on the American Prayer Book* [New York: Seabury Press, 1980], p. 337), specific petitions and thanksgivings would not be inappropriate.

6. See, for example, the readings appointed for Propers 12C and 24C.

7. Other forms, it should be noted, can similarly continue with a Confession (BCP, p. 331 or p. 360), though its connection with the Prayers of the People is obscured because it is located in another part of the Prayer Book and because the Confession is led by a deacon or priest who will usually not have been the leader of the prayers.

8. A significant period of silence before the Celebrant's concluding collect is also desirable as a means of recognizing the place of apophatic prayer in corporate worship.

9. Given the varying degrees of "fit" between a constant Collect and the changing readings of a three-year lectionary, it is probably not a good idea to expect the Collect to provide the structure or content of the sermon. In particular, the Collect should not take precedence over the scriptures but should be regarded as a means of approach to the scriptures. The preacher will often find that daily use of the Collect in personal prayers during the week *before* its liturgical occurrence provides a helpful perspective for reflection on the appointed readings. Fruitful reflections on the Collects can be found in Herbert O'Driscoll's book, *Prayers for the Breaking of Bread: Meditations on the Collects of the Church Year* (Cambridge, MA; Cowley Publications, 1991).

10. See the fine chapter "Preaching as Liturgical Prayer and Sacramental Act," in Patricia Wilson-Kastner, *Imagery for Preaching* (Minneapolis: Fortress Press, 1989), pp. 95–102.